Nuff Said

Also by Tyrus

Just Tyrus: A Memoir

Nuff Said

TYRUS

Post Hill
PRESS

A POST HILL PRESS BOOK
ISBN: 978-1-63758-905-2
ISBN (eBook): 978-1-63758-906-9

Nuff Said
© 2023 by Tyrus
All Rights Reserved

Cover design by Cody Corcoran
Cover photo by Candra George

This is a work of nonfiction. All people, locations, events, and situation are portrayed to the best of the author's memory.

Post Hill Press
New York • Nashville
posthillpress.com

Published in the United States of America
1 2 3 4 5 6 7 8 9 10

I dedicate this book to pain, loss and failure,
the three greatest teachers in life.
You can't win without them.

Table of Contents

Foreword

by Dana Perino

My memory fails me. I can't remember the exact moment I met Tyrus, but I do recall we had an immediate, unspoken connection. It extended far beyond the noticeable height difference between us, him towering a good twenty inches above me. We just *got* each other. He saw me for who I was, and I saw him in return. We could quickly communicate full paragraphs to each other with a single glance. Sometimes it was a simple nod of silent understanding—a gesture acknowledging what the other was thinking. Other times it was a shared pang of empathy. It left others to wonder how we both got into this on-air predicament together. We were like two people bound by a common Gutfeld...separated yet united.

Of course, I had to look up—*way* up—to meet his gaze. The height disparity between us is quite amusing. Words don't do it justice. Allow me to show you. On the next page, there's a photo of us posing in the greenroom before taping an episode of *The Five* back in August 2018. Notice Tyrus had to kneel down...on the floor...on his knees...so that he could stand shoulder-to-shoulder with me.

We also grew up quite differently. I had a stable home with loving parents; a pony on my family's ranch where we spent holidays and summer vacations; family dinners every night; and a plan for my future, which was supported by both my parents and my doting younger sister. Tyrus had none of those things.

As you'll soon read in *Nuff Said*, Tyrus barely survived his turbulent and abusive childhood. He sometimes didn't have enough to eat. He had to dodge blows and heartaches at every turn. He couldn't find a firm foothold from which to launch his dreams. He was a giant who felt very small.

So how did he become the Tyrus we know and love? Perseverance, undoubtedly. Guts, definitely. Determination, no doubt. And a relentless pursuit of happiness—which he has come to realize he deserves.

The little voice in Tyrus's head used to say, "I can't...it's too hard." But now it says, "I will...it's worth fighting for." I bet it also says "put Greg in a headlock" sometimes, but fortunately (or unfortunately?) he's learned to ignore that.

I read *Just Tyrus* in one day. It was so completely honest and vulnerable, moving, and hilarious. I loved the book so much that I told everyone to buy it—and apparently, they did. It was a huge bestseller and allowed Tyrus to share his life story with us. It was fascinating. Heartbreaking. Triumphant. It pushed Tyrus out of his comfort zone and forced him to strip back the layers. And, through that process, he discovered that he is not only a remarkable person, but also a remarkable author.

And now we have *Nuff Said*—his signature phrase, so uniquely him that it probably deserves that little TM trademark symbol after it. In this sequel you'll delve into some of Tyrus's extraordinary life experiences and see how they connect with the most pressing issues of our time: immigration, crime, bullying, athletics, politics, China, parenting, and respect (for ourselves, each other, and the planet). It is Tyrus's commentary on all of these issues that has the power to silence a room. When he talks, people listen. There's so much wisdom and common sense in his takes that you'll finish this book more informed and more optimistic about the future—and we could all use that.

It is an absolute honor to call Tyrus my colleague and my friend. Getting to know him has been a highlight of my life. He lives life large. He makes me laugh, he keeps me humble, and—above all—he reminds me to embrace life with joy, love, and gratitude. I look up to him in more ways than one.

Nuff said.

Dana Perino

Foreword
by Billy Corgan

I first met Tyrus while we both, in sleepier days, were entombed at the second largest professional wrestling company in the world. As designated suit from The Office, I'd been given all the sour apples to manage, and, in that, informed impolitely that this behemoth was among them. So, hat in hand, I approached Tyrus as he sat wrapping hands for a fight he would not have.

"They're booking you wrong," I muttered, throwing away any authority I might hold. "They just don't get who you are or what you are capable of." Tyrus certainly knew by form who I was burying, for his job of late had been to hold another talent's baby in-ring as they spoke, or to mean mug any available camera.

"Well, what would you do?" he asked of the critique.

I cited a forgotten phenom from the past, a stout and unwavering giant who, in being unapologetic for his many gifts, grated positively on one's mind. Yet, as is my custom, I carried on past this winning hand. "And you could also wear a tailored suit."

Shifting his massive frame, Tyrus began to signal our conversation was nearing its fatal end.

"What's your real name?" I broached. My sudden query brought back razor-split eyes.

"George," he'd murmur after an overly long pause.

I continued. "And would you prefer to be called by your real name, or—?" For this impertinence I was coolly sized up. For now, I was offering a hand past all decorum or reason.

"George," said he.

"And your last?"

Almost groaning, George intoned the family name. "It's Murdoch—"

"Are you Scottish?" I had wondered too quick. But this flicked on the megawatt smile that in a year would launch a career in public punditry.

"I am, actually." He laid out the ancestry, which bore our soon-to-be common fruit. "And you?" George wondered politely.

"The same," I confirmed, "amongst other things—"

Knowing Tyrus as I have over this last decade, caught in glimpses and asides and a conversation between us that neither seems to begin or end, I can only share that his success upon the world's stage is of no surprise. For, as owner and CEO of the National Wrestling Alliance, the august brand now in its seventy-fifth year of continuous operation, I am often witness to the show behind the show. Where a proud father might weep with his children in arms as he absorbs the magnitude of being just crowned World Champion or kibbutz with those he broke in the business with not as star, but as equal.

This, you might see, is a place beyond politic and beyond every other manner of divide. For this is the stuff of love and triumph over that which might just as easily have dragged another under; and for good. And, of that man, I am proud.

William Patrick Corgan

6-21-23

Introduction

When my first book, *Just Tyrus*, came out last April, I really didn't know what to expect. I was proud of it, I was hoping my friends and family would read it, but, beyond that, I had no real expectations.

The day it was released, it hit number one on Amazon and sat there for the entire week. Number one on Barnes & Noble. Kindle. Out of stock everywhere. Forty thousand copies. Poof. Gone. Not knowing too much about the publishing industry, I wasn't sure quite what to make of this. Was it as big a deal as some people were saying? I guess so.

I'd be lying if I told you it didn't catch me off guard and give me pause. I'm competitive. I like to win. But this was not my game. This was my first rodeo. And I found myself sitting on top of a bucking bronco. My associates at Fox News were excited and supportive. That meant a lot to me. Then I started reading the hundreds of reviews that popped up on Amazon in the first couple of days. That's when I realized that my story connected with people. People weren't just buying the book and reading it. They were devouring it. And then they were sharing their feelings. Whatever struggles they were going through in their lives, my story was resonating with them and helping them cope with their challenges. I was just sharing my story. I had no idea it would have this kind of effect on people. If you've watched me on Fox News, you know I like to try to be funny, I'm fairly confident in my ability to comment on current events, and I'm not shy, but this experience with *Just Tyrus* humbled me. When my son sent me a video of him picking up the book up in his local Barnes & Noble, I broke down in tears. That made it real.

Every interview I did to promote the book, I realized that everyone talking to me had actually read it. A lot of times in television, an assistant will jot some notes down because, often times, the hosts don't have time to read. It seemed that everybody I spoke to had read *Just Tyrus*. I had been so nervous right before the book came out because it felt like maybe I was oversharing. I was getting naked in front of people and, all of a sudden, I wasn't sure if I was comfortable with that. Then I realized: that stripped-down honesty is what people were reacting to.

With that realization, I knew I had to keep writing. I have more stories about the arc of my life, and I've also got plenty of real takes on what's happening in the world today. Things we really need to talk about as a nation.

So here we go. I'm ready to keep sharing, to keep getting to the heart and soul of what matters to lots of people who are scared, frustrated, confused, and just looking for some common sense in an increasingly caustic and chaotic world. I have no idea what will happen with this book.

But I'm ready to find out.

Just a note about the content here. What I intend to do is address a current societal issue in each chapter and then add a story from my life that relates to that issue. Pretty simple formula. My hope is that maybe you can begin to think about your

CHAPTER 1

Stand-Up

Since my first book came out last year, I have embarked on kind of a stand-up comedy career. Lots of storytelling. Hot takes. Basically what I do on television but blown up into ninety minutes. To say that it's been a revelation would be an understatement. The reviews are unbelievable. I do a meet and greet afterward, and fans are just like, "We didn't know what to expect, but we had no idea it was going to be like this. This is the best comedy show I've ever been to. I haven't seen anything like this since Robin Williams."

Whaaaaaat?

When I ended up on *Gutfeld!*, it basically was a chance for me to do my improv on the subjects of the day. And it just kept growing and growing. At one point, Greg said to me, "If you start doing stand-up, I would lose you in a year."

That meant a lot to me because he knows funny. The more I contributed to the show, the more laughs I heard myself getting, and it really got me thinking about where I could take my act, so to speak. I watch a lot of comedy on TV, and I have to admit, sometimes I wonder how that person got on the screen. I'm not being a hater. I would just question how certain things happened. I appreciate great comedy, but there were definitely people I saw on television that I thought I might be funnier than. That gave me hope. *If they can do it, why can't I?*

But I still didn't have the confidence to get out there and do it. It's a big move. And I'm a big guy. I mean, physically big. That was part of my insecurity. Was I too physically big to get up on stage to try and be funny? Would I be like Shrek up there? Would I feel like a train wreck before I even opened my mouth? I needed something to happen to create an opportunity.

Thankfully, when Greg was doing one of his book-signing shows, he invited me to appear with him, just come out and have some small talk with him in front of the audience. Me being me, once I had that microphone in my hand, I just started riffing, making up jokes on the spot and telling a few stories. The place was dying. I saw people laughing as hard as they knew how to laugh. Right then, a switch flipped inside of me. Afterward, my wife, Ingrid, came up to me and said, "You need to do your own shows. You need to do your own stand-up. That entire audience of people was laughing their asses off with you." She knows me pretty well. She has seen me in many different situations. And she was definitely picking up on something special.

So, I decided to quietly give it a shot. I would use a fake name and go in to a few places around the country and just get up there and do a few minutes, try to get a few laughs. I felt like I had accomplished a lot in wrestling. I was in the middle of accomplishing a lot on television. Then I started getting that thing that people sometimes get, like the actor who wants to be a singer, or a singer who wants to be an actor, and so forth. I've seen it happen before as an observer. Sometimes it works, sometimes it doesn't. But there was only one way to find out. I had to get out there and do it on a regular basis. I had to start channeling my inner Richard Pryor.

I listened to Richard Pryor practically every day of my childhood. When my mom worked nights, he kept me company in the dark. I knew every routine of his by heart. I listen to his *Live on the Sunset Strip* album every time before I take the stage. It's like getting a pep talk from a dad I never had. And I still laugh at his jokes because of the timing, the social relevance, and that unique Richard Pryor energy.

Things started to pick up. It became easier to book shows. But then the insecurity kicked in. I was thinking to myself, *There's no way anybody is going to buy tickets to see me. They can see me on television for free every night. What business do I have doing a stand-up comedy show that requires people to purchase tickets?* I was just being real with myself. In my youth, oftentimes when I failed, I would look to blame anybody else but me. One thing I quickly realized doing stand-up is, it's you and you alone up there. If you fail, there's nobody to blame but yourself. Was I prepared for this? Was I prepared for the worst? Was I going to be able to handle it if I went out there in front of a large audience, cracked some jokes, and heard nothing but the sound of silence in response? It was a huge risk. I understand that pain and loss and failure are good teachers, but I also understand that sometimes you shouldn't set yourself up for failure if you're not able to handle the consequences. I felt that I could, but I wasn't quite sure. Then the shows began to sell out. I should have been thrilled about that, which I was to a degree, but the amount of pressure that I'd created overwhelmed the excitement.

I believe the first really big venue that I did on my own that sold out quickly was in St. Louis. I was sitting backstage thinking to myself that I had not written one joke for the show. I was going on in a few hours and I needed to figure something out quickly. I love the idea of performing stand-up as an abstract concept, but I had not given it the proper thought that I needed to create and fine-tune an actual act. My whole persona and television personality was all about shooting from the hip and being off the cuff. It works terrific in little bursts when you are sitting on a panel with other smart funny people, but it's a bit different when you're about to go out and face two thousand people who are expecting a great show because they paid good money for it in a tough economy. How could I have forgotten to polish my act before doing my first big sold-out show?

I needed to figure something out quickly. I took a pad of paper, and I wrote individual words down on that top sheet. That was my outline. I wasn't going to write a script or tell myself what to say, I just provided a few trigger words to help me remember some fun stories and jokes that were floating around my head. Everybody has their own style; this was mine.

There was more pressure on me. I would be wrestling for the NWA Heavyweight Championship against Trevor Murdoch in the next couple of days and so I had invited some wrestlers to come down and catch the show. Everyone I invited came to support me. Billy Corgan came to the show. As you probably know, he's an extremely accomplished and successful musician, the founder of the legendary Smashing Pumpkins, and also the owner of the NWA.

Before the show, I put on my headphones, cranked up Richard Pryor, and got into my groove. Then I went out there for about ninety minutes and brought the house down by simply looking down at that little list of words. To this day, I still don't write much down before a show, just little words to guide me. That night kind of changed my world. It gave me the faith and the hope that I could really do this in front of people and succeed. Not every night was killer, but the more I did it the more consistent the positive audience reactions became, which just fueled me even more. The events kept getting bigger, they started selling out faster, and I noticed that I was even connecting more during my television appearances. My confidence was up, I had some extra swagger, and I felt that my chops as an entertainer were becoming far more polished thanks to my new stand-up gig.

I love to deal with the occasional hecklers because that takes me back to my wrestling one-liner talents, which is really where I live—quick, pointed comebacks. After the shows, at the meet and greets, people would tell me that while they thought the stories and jokes were funny, they also found them touching and relatable. This is when *Just Tyrus* was starting to blow up, and I began feeling a much deeper sense of connection to the audience. When you sit there on television, you really don't know who is watching at home. At these shows, however, all of a sudden, I began to get a real sense of what the audience was all about. These were, in large part, down-to-earth, smart, funny people who were just looking for a little bit of escape from the bullshit. They were happy to be out in public watching a live event. And they were just as happy that I joked about things that probably drive them a little bit crazy in this world, from politics to everyday life. Although I don't hit politics too hard in the act. Just a passing comment here and there. It's really not about politics. It's about getting through life.

All of a sudden, my size didn't matter. In fact, it kind of became an asset because I was such an anomaly. Think about it. Comedians in general are not that physically imposing. For the most part, they're just like regular people. I'm like a freak show up there physically, but people seem to like that I talk common-sense comedy that hits them where they live. In a very real way, doing stand-up began to feel like my true calling in life. Sort of like everything I have been preparing for since childhood. My sense of timing, my ability to tell a story, and how much I loved cracking wise with people suddenly had a much deeper purpose. I began catching myself before I went out there on stage. *Is this really happening? There are people sitting in the back row. A full house. And everybody seems to be there for the same and right reason. To laugh. To get away from the bullshit.*

Many times in my life I had put up roadblocks when I thought I couldn't achieve something. That was me. I would convince myself I couldn't do something. Now, the exact opposite was happening. I think a lot of us put up roadblocks. We convince ourselves that we can't do something over some stupid detail that only we see. *Oh, I can't take this job because I have kids! Oh, I can't do this job because I was a C student in college.* Even though it's only our own personal reality. It's not real. We have no way of knowing what we can do unless we actually go out there and do it. If I go out and crack jokes and nobody laughs and I barely get polite applause, then I know I need to get better or get off the stage. I felt proud of myself for stepping out of my box and trying something new. If it didn't work, it would still be a victory because I had tried something bold and learned something about myself.

Being on stage has become an escape for me. Any hassles in life that I may be having at the time completely disappear when I take that stage. Nobody can get me after. It's the ultimate safety zone. It's like wrestling in a way. You get yourself up and up and up for the show, and then it's over and the rush is gone. You didn't have to bring yourself down. I know, for certain entertainers, we need to artificially get ourselves in the mood with either drugs or alcohol. But for me, the Art of performing is the drug itself. It's what gets me high. It's what gives me purpose. In a way, it's what defines me.

When I read positive reviews of my shows, and when famous people come backstage to see me and complement the show, it's very humbling. I do not take any of this for granted. I don't think I have a big head, especially when I'm getting ready to go out onstage. In fact, I'm always a little bit nervous. Call them butterflies, call them whenever you want, I have them. But once the curtains open, it's like the ring of the bell in a match. It's just me and the audience. It's so raw. I have to figure out what the mood of the crowd is. I'm creating a relationship with them, and I like to nurture that. Then, for an hour and a half, we can laugh together and talk about stuff that we can't talk about anywhere else. I'm always reminded of what my wrestling mentor, Dusty Rhodes, said to me years ago. "I don't worry about you, kid, because when you smell the popcorn and you hear the crowd, you will always know what to do."

That seems to come naturally to me, unlike personal relationships and parenting: things you really have to work at every day no matter what. Even if it feels natural it still requires lots of working energy. But entertainment? It just feels like what I'm born to do. Especially in front of a live audience. I hope you get to come to see one of my shows sometime. But more than that, when you leave, I hope you have a sense that you can do anything you put your mind to. I hope my shows help you believe a little bit more in yourself and even encourage you to take a shot at something you would not normally be taking a shot at. That's what life's about. Failing is fine. You will learn from that if things don't work out once you take the shot. More often than not, I believe you will find there's victory simply in trying. And when things do connect and you succeed and everything works out, well, I'm here to tell you, that truly is like a little bit of heaven on earth.

It all started for me when I was in the ninth grade, when I had first been introduced to Mr. Rivera, my drama teacher, who was bringing me in because I was considered a troubled youth. I had just been pulled out of sports by my stepfather. I was having a rough time at home. I just was kind of lost and having a really hard time finding any kind of voice or purpose. I hated going home. I hated going to school. My friendships weren't really friendships anymore because I was so withdrawn all the time. You live in a constant state of...just fear because I was always one comment away from a backhand. I was one look away from a punch or being grounded. I was just unhappy. And there was nowhere for me to go. So my grades were suffering, and I was looking for another elective. That's when Mr. Rivera goes, "You should try the drama class."

I took his advice. So now I'm going to do drama class with Mr. Rivera. Honestly, in many ways, that saved my life. Not in a melodramatic sense, like it kept me from offing myself, but it gave me a sense of purpose, a place to be special, powerful, unique, and different. Before Mr. Rivera's class, I was definitely the class clown, always making jokes and always getting in trouble for it. I was known for being a smart-ass and a bad student. But then Mr. Rivera introduced me to a game called Freeze. It starts with two people on a stage playing out a scene until somebody yells "freeze." Then another student comes onto the stage, taps one of the people on the shoulder to replace them, and then introduces an entirely different scenario. It might start off with two people driving away to vacation and then someone yells freeze, and the next thing you know, we're now at the doctor's office sitting in the waiting room.

It was a fun game. I was pretty self-conscious at first, so I would never volunteer to take part. I would sit in the back and basically try not to be noticed. I wasn't outgoing at all. I didn't have the self-esteem or confidence yet. I think Mr. Rivera realized that, so he encouraged me to get involved, which I eventually did. My situation at home, with my mom's abusive boyfriend Craig constantly beating me down, really made things bad at this point in my life. Again, Mr. Rivera seemed to sense something else was going on, so he went out of his way to engage me. I would watch these kids playing Freeze and think to myself, *That's not funny. Why are they all laughing? Why is everyone having such a good time?* One thing when you're miserable is that you love to find the flaws in everything. Misery loves company. I was being an asshole. If I wanted to laugh, I could go home and just watch Richard Pryor.

After a few weeks, Mr. Rivera insisted that I come up to the head of the class and start a game of Freeze. I was terrified. I had been avoiding it so much. I still give him so much credit. He didn't put pressure on me right away. He waited a few weeks. A lot of other teachers might have tried to force me into that spot much earlier, and they would have lost me immediately because I would have pushed back. I would have created a power struggle with them. I already had no power at home, so I was trying to get as much as I could in class, which is not a good place to be. Anyway, I go to the front of the class with another student, and he gave us a situation to act out. We were supposed to be at a table in a restaurant when we both realize that we don't have our wallets. How were we going to pay for dinner? We're sitting there, and I was pretending like I was eating. And then we got the check I looked up and I said, "Oh, I'll take the check." The other kid says, "Oh, I'll take the check." I said, "No, I'll take the check," then "Give me the check. I took the check and reached for my back pocket. I did the thing where I made my eyes big, and a couple of kids giggled. I checked both my back pockets and my front pockets, and I looked at him and said, "You know what? You're right. You should take the check." He was like, "Sure." He checks his pocket and is like, "You know what? Maybe you should." Then some kid yelled, "Freeze!" I was pissed. I was like, *We didn't even get to the best part of it*. Of course, they walked up, tagged me, and I'm off. Now, I'm mad.

Because. I was feeling it. I was liking this. I had gotten a laugh. It wasn't a huge laugh, but it was enough for me. That feeling of accomplishment or that feeling of, for lack of a better word, power, the ability to change the temperature of the room. I did it with just a facial expression and grabbing my butt, looking for a wallet that wasn't there. I liked that moment of being able to take a group of people and make them laugh or make them think a certain way. It was like a vitamin shot of confidence. I went, sat down, waited maybe two turns, and raised my hand. Mr. Rivera called me up, and I came back on the stage. This time it was with a girl.

As soon as I got up there, I started hopping up and down like I had to use the bathroom, knocking on the door. She started saying, "I'm almost done," and I was saying to her, "Well, what the heck are you doing? This is taking forever!" People in the class were dying laughing because let's face it, bathroom jokes in the ninth grade are hilarious. And the girl is getting embarrassed because I didn't think about her feelings. Today I would probably be in trouble for that. This went on and on for a while, and afterward Mr. Rivera pulled me aside and said, "You know what, you're a funny guy. You don't smile a lot in class, but you're a funny guy."

Mr. Rivera encouraged me and he pushed me. After about a month, nobody would tap me on the shoulder to get me to leave the stage. When I got called up for Freeze, I was up there for the whole episode because everybody wanted to work with me. After all, I was going to say something funny and make them look good. It just kind of built and built. Then one day Mr. Rivera told me there was a school talent show and said, "You need to do this. You need to do some stand-up comedy." That blew my mind. Outside of doing some Richard Pryor impersonations, I knew nothing about stand-up comedy. The drama class was a very private space where we learned about acting and plays and improvisation. Doing stand-up was going to be an entirely different thing. Obviously, it would just be me up there. But if he believed in me, I was ready for that challenge. A big school play was also happening at that time, and Mr. Rivera had me playing three different characters: the sheriff, the town drunk, and an old man. There was also a part he wanted me to play in drag, which I pushed back on, but he said to me, "You have to do this. It's going to challenge you. If you want to be a better actor and comedian, you have to take risks." I noticed that being in the drama class helped with my other classes because I was growing confident as a person. It even helped with my sports because again, I believed more in myself with everything Mr. Rivera was putting me through.

When it came time to rehearse my act for the talent show, Mr. Rivera was right there with me. I had written a bunch of things about being a frustrated ninth grader and he thought I was funny. Long story short, I won the talent show, in part on the strength of a couple of very strong urination jokes. Ninth grade, remember? Always go with the bathroom humor. That earned me a visit from the vice principal. I will never forget this. He pulled me aside and said, "You are going to be famous one day. But please, no more jokes about peeing." I was like, "Yes, sir."

The vice principal told me about an acting school in Los Angeles that he thought I might thrive in if I wanted to change schools. He told me it was my calling. Unfortunately, my mother and Craig did not see the merit in me going to a school that didn't really have sports, plus it was going to cost a fair amount of tuition, even if was my calling. And so I packed those dreams away. Of course, back then I had no idea what the future held. And I knew no matter what, if I was ever going to make it on stage as a performer, particularly doing comedy, that it was going to take a lot of work and a lot of luck. But I had people in my corner. I had a great teacher and a vice principal who believed in me.

My love for comedy came from the joy it brought to people's lives. There was nothing quite like the feeling of making someone laugh and seeing their face light up with happiness.

I knew that if I could become a successful comedian, I would be able to bring that joy to thousands of people.

Over the years, I spent countless hours watching stand-up comedy specials, studying the craft and learning from the best in the business. I spend hours writing and refining my own jokes, experimenting with different styles and techniques. I practiced in front of the mirror, trying out different voices and mannerisms until I found what worked. The road to success was long and difficult, but I never lost sight of my goal. I knew that if I kept working hard and never gave up, I would eventually achieve my dream of becoming a successful stand-up comedian.

Looking back on my journey, I realize that my passion for comedy was not just a passing phase. It was a calling that I had felt since I was a child, and it was a part of who I was. Even when it seemed like the odds were stacked against me, I never gave up on my dream. I knew that becoming a stand-up comedian was my destiny, and I was never going to let go of that dream.

High school is a critical time in a young person's life, where they are beginning to explore their interests and passions and think about their future career path. Navigating this process can be overwhelming and confusing, which is why having mentors to guide and support them is so important. Mentors can be teachers, coaches, family members, or professionals in the student's desired field. They can provide valuable insight, advice, and support to help the student make informed decisions about their future. In addition to providing practical guidance, mentors can also offer emotional support and encouragement. High school can be a challenging and stressful time, and having someone to turn to for guidance and support can make all the difference. Mentors can help students develop resilience and perseverance, which are critical skills for success in any career path.

Mr. Rivera, and my old vice principal, if you're out there reading this book, thank you for seeing something in me when I was in high school. Without you, your encouragement, and your support, I would never be where I am today.

CHAPTER 2

Frederick Douglass

Frederick Douglass (1818–1895) was an American social reformer, abolitionist, orator, writer, and statesman. He was born into slavery in Maryland and escaped to the North in 1838. After gaining his freedom, Douglass became a prominent figure in the abolitionist movement, speaking out against the institution of slavery and advocating for the rights of African Americans.

Douglass is best known for his powerful speeches and writings, which exposed the brutality and injustice of slavery and inspired many to join the fight for abolition. In his auto-biographical works, including *Narrative of the Life of Frederick Douglass, an American Slave* (1845), he gave firsthand accounts of the horrors of slavery, challenging the prevailing belief that enslaved people were content with their lot.

Douglass also played an important role in the women's suffrage movement, advocating for the right to vote for all women, regardless of race. He was the only African American to attend the Seneca Falls Convention in 1848, where he delivered a speech in support of women's rights.

Throughout his life, Douglass remained committed to the cause of social justice, fighting against slavery, racism, and discrimination. He served as a statesman and diplomat, representing the United States as a consul to Haiti and, later, as a minister-resident to the Dominican Republic.

Today, Frederick Douglass is remembered as a hero and a symbol of the struggle for equality and human rights. His legacy continues to inspire and empower those fighting for social justice and equality.

And he is my hero.

He was a man of substance we seem to have forgotten. That's unfortunate because when that happens, we stop learning from him.

No one in my generation has confronted the challenges he did. But when you listen to the "struggles" that some people claim to be facing today, you would think our world is a tougher place than it was in the days of Frederick Douglass. It's not.

As a country, we have succeeded in progressing to a point where we focus on things that no other country needs to focus on—issues that aren't real to anyone but ourselves. In that respect, we are spoiled. We argue about pronouns. Think about that. Not true racism.

There's education and opportunities available to just about anybody if you're willing to do the work. That wasn't the case in the days of Frederick Douglass. There were laws preventing people from being equal. We don't have that any longer, despite with some people would have you believe.

We've gotten to the point where everybody is so safe and secure in general that we have forgotten what real struggles are.

I'm not saying there is no more racism. I'm saying that it's no longer systemic and an institutionalized problem that some people on the left would have you believe it is. We make excuses today. We create problems that don't even really exist. Well, *they* do, anyway.

What would Frederick Douglass think about the fact that recently, while I was writing this book, the University of Southern California (in part) banned the word "field" from certain usages in their studies. They determined that the word may now be seen as racist. The word "field" is not a problem. Idiots who decide the word "field" is the problem are the problem.

I often wonder what Frederick Douglass would think about the country today. I work in the entertainment field. Nobody should be offended by that statement. "In the summer I used to walk my dog in a field of grass." With the exception of maybe some people who suffer from hay fever, nobody should take issue with that statement. "My great grandfather was a field hand."

NPR reported that an office at University of Southern California's School of Social Work was removing the term "field" from its curriculum because it may have racist connotations related to slavery.

"This change supports anti-racist social work practice by replacing language that could be considered anti-Black or anti-immigrant in favor of inclusive language," the memo reads. "Language can be powerful, and phrases such as 'going into the field' or 'field work' may have connotations for descendants of slavery and immigrant workers that are not benign."

The change at the USC school comes as a growing number of entities take steps to remove terminology with ties to slavery or racism. Within the computer science field, some people are ditching terms like "master" and "slave," while the Girl Guides of Canada recently renamed its "Brownies" branch.

Mildred Joyner, the president of National Association of Social Workers (NASW), said she applauds the USC office for its change—and while she isn't aware of other universities doing the same, she disagrees with those that say the office is going too far.

"I don't know what going too far means," she said. "Does that mean going too far to treat people with dignity and respect and remove all language that oppresses people? Then kudos to that department."

Where does this insanity end? Will the word "cotton" soon be deemed too racist? So we will not be able to say cotton candy? Or cotton swab? This slope isn't just slippery, it's steep, it's unmarked, and it's endless.

These are the things we worry about now. Not true equality. Not true civil rights. We worry about policing speech. I don't think this is what Frederick Douglass was fighting for.

Something else that fascinates me about Frederick Douglass. He always kept shoes right by his bed so he could be prepared for whatever was happening next. And he worked out. He was never without a set of weights. That was important to him. Being ready and being in shape both mentally and physically.

He had a routine; he had a vision. That's what I admire most about him. Planning. In my life, having a plan has always been the path to success.

When I first heard that the WWE was going to offer me a contract, I knew I needed a plan. I knew what my goal was: to get a contract. So I put together a plan. I was going to get up every morning and go straight to the gym. I had my clothes and my gym membership card and my clothes laid out the night before. As soon as I got up, I knew what my day was going to be. There were no excuses. I eliminated all of the things that could have created excuses. I wanted something. I needed that to happen, so I knew I needed a plan. Now, obviously, Frederick Douglass did these things for different reasons. He was carrying the weight of a culture on his back. And he was leading a slave nation toward freedom, against all odds. I was just trying to get a wrestling contract. But being inspired by someone doesn't mean the stakes have to be the same. I learned from his example. We can all learn from that example, black or white, or whatever you happen to be.

Frederick Douglass had to be mentally and physically fit every day because he never knew if somebody was going to come at him and try and kill him. The reasons for him to be more prepared far exceeded mine. But again, it's the principles that we learn from.

A pair of shoes and two dumbbells by his bed. I can't think of any more impactful symbols throughout American history that have affected me more than those.

I think the biggest lesson with men like Frederick Douglas is that he took his life in his own hands every time he spoke up. Think of that kind of courage. Think about what we can learn from that. He was respected because of his intellect, but think about what he had to overcome as a Black man.

I'm able to do what I do today because of people like Frederick Douglass. And I think Frederick Douglass would be shocked to hear people on the left pontificating that the country is no better today than it was when he was alive. To hear people talk about how oppressive everything is, how racist this country is. Those who say that are basically arguing

'Nuff Said

SJWs

They make me nuts. Self-anointed "Social Justice Warriors" who look to disrupt society on all kinds of levels.

First, let's define what an SJW is. Social justice warriors are individuals who are extremely vocal about their beliefs in social justice issues such as racism, sexism, homophobia, transphobia, and other forms of oppression. While fighting for social justice is a noble cause, the methods used by SJWs often lead to more harm than good.

One of the biggest dangers of SJWs is their tendency to engage in cancel culture. Cancel culture is the act of boycotting or ostracizing individuals or groups who hold different beliefs or opinions. SJWs often use cancel culture as a way to silence those who disagree with them or challenge their ideas, even if those individuals are not necessarily harmful or offensive. This kind of behavior is dangerous because it stifles free speech and creates an environment where people are afraid to express their thoughts and opinions for fear of being cancelled.

Another danger of SJWs is their tendency to engage in virtue signaling. Virtue signaling is the act of publicly expressing one's moral or ethical values in order to gain approval or praise from others. SJWs often engage in virtue signaling by using social media platforms to publicly denounce anything they deem as "problematic" or "offensive." While this may seem harmless, it can lead to a toxic culture where people are more concerned with appearing morally superior than actually doing good in the world.

One of the biggest issues with SJWs is their tendency to create a victim mentality. SJWs often view themselves as oppressed victims and see the world as divided into two groups: the oppressed and the oppressors. They believe that anyone who does not share their views is automatically part of the oppressor group, regardless of their actual beliefs or actions. This kind of thinking is dangerous because it creates a culture where people are judged solely on their identity rather than their individual merits.

In addition to creating a victim mentality, SJWs often engage in identity politics. Identity politics is the practice of organizing political or social movements around specific identity categories such as race, gender, or sexual orientation. While identity politics can be useful in raising awareness about systemic oppression, SJWs often take it to an extreme by promoting a "my group versus your group" mentality. This kind of thinking is dangerous because it creates division and can lead to a society that is more concerned with identity than with individual merit.

SJWs also often engage in what is known as "microaggressions." Microaggressions are subtle and often unintentional forms of discrimination that can be harmful to marginalized groups. While it's important to address and eliminate micro-aggressions, SJWs often take it to an extreme by labeling any behavior or speech that they deem as "problematic" as a microaggression. This kind of thinking is dangerous because it leads to a culture of hypersensitivity where people are afraid to speak or act for fear of offending someone.

It's essential to recognize that not everyone who disagrees with you is automatically your enemy or part of the oppressor group. It's possible to have productive discussions and debates with people who hold different beliefs, and it's important to approach these discussions with an open mind and a willingness to listen and learn.

While social justice warriors may have good intentions, their methods often lead to more harm than good. It's important to recognize the dangers of cancel culture, virtue signaling, victim mentality, identity politics, and hypersensitivity, and to engage in critical thinking and open dialogue in order to effect real change in the world. In the end, maybe just remember basic respect and responsibility when you were dealing with people. It's not just about you. It's about listening. It's about manners. It's about basic decency when it comes to communication.

Nuff said.

CHAPTER 3

Meet Me in the Middle

The original title for this book was *Meet Me in the Middle*. My thinking was, I'm not about extremes. In my opinion, extremes are what are causing the majority of problems in this country today. I'm not crazy about the term "compromise," but it does become important when you debate. You don't always have to compromise, but I do think you have to consider it sometimes. Meeting in the middle can be a valuable approach to finding common ground with your adversaries.

In recent years, the political divide between the right and the left has grown increasingly pronounced. Political polarization has become a topic of concern for many, as it has led to a lack of cooperation, gridlock in government, and an inability to address pressing issues. That's why I want to explore the importance of seeking political compromise between the right and the left, and why it is crucial for the health and well-being of our country.

Compromise is an essential element of a functioning democracy. In a democracy, people with differing opinions and beliefs come together to form a government that represents the will of the people. Right? The government must then make decisions that benefit the entire society, not just one particular group. Compromise is the only way to achieve this goal.

Compromise is not about giving up one's beliefs or principles. Instead, it is about finding common ground and working towards a solution that benefits all parties involved. Compromise requires empathy, understanding, and a willingness to listen to opposing viewpoints. It is a skill that must be honed and practiced, but the benefits are immense.

Political polarization occurs when people with different political beliefs become unwilling to compromise. This polarization has become increasingly pronounced in recent years, with people on the right and left becoming more entrenched in their beliefs and less willing to entertain or sympathize with opposing perspectives. The dangers of political polarization are clear. When people become more polarized, they are less likely to work together towards common goals. We see it every day. This has led to gridlock in government, making it difficult to pass legislation. It can also lead to a lack of trust in government and a sense of disillusionment with the political process for people on the left and right.

There are many benefits to seeking political compromise between the right and the left. First and foremost, compromise allows for progress. When people are willing to work together and find common ground, they are more likely to achieve meaningful results.

Compromise also promotes understanding and empathy. When people are willing to listen to opposing viewpoints and work towards a solution, they develop a greater understanding of the concerns and needs of others. This empathy can help to bridge the divide between different groups and promote greater unity.

Compromise also promotes stability. When people are willing to compromise, they are less likely to engage in extreme actions that could destabilize the political system. This stability is essential for the functioning of a democracy, as it allows for the peaceful transfer of power and the maintenance of the rule of law. Any politicians reading this following me now?

Finally, compromise promotes respect. When people are willing to compromise, they show respect for others and their beliefs. This respect is essential for the functioning of a democracy, as it allows for a free and open exchange of ideas without fear of retribution.

Seeking political compromise is not always easy, but I believe there are steps that can be taken to promote greater unity and understanding between the right and the left. Basic shit. Shit I teach my kids. The first step is to listen to opposing viewpoints. When people are willing to listen to others and understand their concerns, they are more likely to find common ground.

The second step is to find common ground. When people are willing to look for areas of agreement, they are more likely to achieve meaningful results. This can involve finding solutions that benefit both parties or compromising on certain issues in order to achieve a larger goal.

The third step is to be willing to make concessions. Compromise requires a willingness from both parties to give something up in order to achieve a larger goal. This means that people must be willing to put aside their own self-interests and focus on the greater good.

The fourth step is to communicate effectively. Effective communication is essential for finding common ground and promoting understanding between the right and the left. This means that people must be willing to engage in civil discourse and respect the opinions of others, even when they disagree.

Finally, seeking political compromise requires leadership. Leaders must be willing to put aside their own self-interest and work towards solutions that benefit the entire society. They must also be willing to take risks and make tough decisions in order to achieve meaningful results.

Look, seeking political compromise between the right and the left is essential for the health and well-being of our democracy. Compromise allows for progress to be made, promotes understanding and empathy, promotes stability, promotes respect, and requires leadership. While seeking compromise can be a challenge, it is essential for the functioning of a successful democracy. As citizens, we must be willing to listen to opposing viewpoints, find common ground, make concessions, communicate effectively, and demand leadership from our elected officials. Only then can we achieve a society that is truly united and working towards the greater good.

Meeting someone in the middle politically takes guts because it requires individuals to step outside of their comfort zones and challenge their own beliefs and values. When people hold strong political beliefs, they often feel a deep sense of conviction about their ideas and may see compromise as a betrayal of their principles.

Meeting someone in the middle politically requires a willingness to listen to opposing viewpoints, considering alternative perspectives, and seeking common ground. This can be difficult and uncomfortable, as it may involve setting aside personal biases and prejudices. It also requires individuals to be open-minded and flexible, which can be challenging for those who are set in their ways.

Meeting someone in the middle politically may involve making concessions or compromising on certain issues. This may require individuals to give up something they hold dear in order to achieve a larger goal. It gets risky, too, as compromising on certain issues may lead to criticism or backlash from those who do not agree with the decision.

In addition, meeting someone in the middle politically requires individuals to engage in civil discourse and respectful communication. It also means that individuals must be willing to listen and consider opposing viewpoints without becoming defensive or dismissive.

Bottom line, meeting someone in the middle politically takes courage because it requires individuals to be open-minded and flexible, make concessions, and engage in civil discourse and respectful communication. It requires individuals to challenge their own beliefs and values, and to be willing to work towards solutions that benefit the entire society, not just one particular group. Does it always work? No. Is it worth trying. Hell yes.

I've been meeting people in the middle my entire life. I've always had to compromise.

That's part of being a man in this country. Most of the time, you don't get your way, you don't get what you want to do. You do what you have to do and hope you get to a point in your life to where you can do everything you want to do. In the meantime, to keep doing the things you have to do, you have to compromise with the things that you want to do.

I wanted to play football in college. I worked my ass off all through high school to get there. The same applied to working and just trying to figure out the way the world works. It's a path traveled by millions of people trying to get ahead in life. Some of us make it, and some of us don't. Often, it's the ones who are willing to compromise who make it. Not necessarily always. And I'm not talking in terms of your belief systems. But a lot of times those are tested too.

Any time you walk into a situation where you are working for someone, whether it's Arby's or Fox News, you're going to have to compromise, because it's not your company. You're not the boss. You will observe the guidelines and the aspirations of the people above you, so you better learn quickly to compromise, or you will not have a lot of long-term jobs. Compromise is the greatest way to learn wisdom.

When I was bodyguarding Snoop Dogg, everything was a compromise. He was paying me to protect him, watch out for him, get him to his appointments, run his programs—whatever he needed done. I got paid well, but my beliefs, my wants, the things I wanted to do, were no longer relevant.

I worked for Snoop. I was helping him live his best life, and I was watching him live his best life.

One of the problems I used to have was getting Snoop to places on time, because when you are a person of his stature, you can stop time. Most of the time, he didn't have to compromise just because of who he is. He's at that point. He's earned that right.

I couldn't go up to him and be like, "Hey man, stop being late. You're making me look bad." I'd have been fired.

But I'm an alpha-type male, so I had to find a way to communicate without coming off as aggressive or angry. This is another key aspect of meeting in the middle.

You have to be able to outsource.

You have to reach out for help, and you have to be honest with yourself.

I did the best thing that I could do. I went to his manager, Kevin Barkey, and I said, "Listen, we both need to come together and find ways that we can get Snoop to the places that we need to get him on time so we can make sure he gets everywhere he needs to go."

Kevin said, "You know what? You're the first bodyguard to come to me with this. So what do we want? What are you thinking?"

I was like, "Well, if we work together, we can meet in the morning to review his schedule and see what the key things are. If his schedule says he has a music video at eleven, we tell him it's at ten."

Kevin looked at me like, "Okay. Fuck it. Let's do it together.

So that's what we did. We began concocting little schemes to get him up and out earlier, tricking him into being punctual. We knew we had to build in a couple of hours of "Snoop time" because he just runs late. But now, for the most part, he was getting places on time, and I was able to do my job.

Here's the thing. You never want to be confronted by the person you are working for. These kinds of compromises help reduce the opportunities for confrontation.

Meeting in the middle became very effective while working with Snoop. He not only wasn't late anymore, he was actually showing up early for some things. Total win-win.

We also left our egos at home, which is important when you're going to meet somebody in the middle, because here's the deal. Somebody is going to want to take credit for this. Somebody wants to take credit for this, or worse, if it goes bad and he's pissed, someone's going to want to blame somebody because they see it as an opportunity for themselves to get ahead.

Just like that cancel culture stuff.

They're going to try to use your situation to further themselves, even though they don't have the ability to do what you are doing.

It's a very, very slippery slope when you're dealing with situations where it can't be "your" way and you have to work with someone else or other people to get where you need to go.

With Snoop, the biggest problem was making sure he got on planes on time. This is when you're doing a million things a day, as he was. He was extremely busy and rarely slept because he was just nonstop. In that situation, you're going to have days where you don't want to travel, you know, because you're a millionaire, and it's like. "Well, it's not like I need the money."

So you have to find ways to get him where he needs to be. Me kicking in the door like, "Yo, get your skinny ass up, Snoop," is not going to work. What will work is finding something in the middle.

It works great 99 percent of the time. But, inevitably, there's always that one time it doesn't come off. Kevin and I were working hard together to make sure Snoop was on time for his many appointments and appearances. I can't stress enough, Snoop is so famous and so iconic, it's difficult to describe how much planning is involved in his daily life. It's amazing how he keeps it all together. It's one of the things I love most about him.

But this one time, they wanted him to come to a recording studio for some event, and I didn't realize that the studio was only a couple of minutes from his house. We had moved the time up an hour, but we got there an hour early and they weren't ready for him. The other performer wasn't there yet, and Snoop did this slow look at Kevin like, "Why the fuck are we here? I could be playing *Madden* right now." Because I had screwed up with the address, now we were wasting the boss's time. He didn't like that, and I don't blame him. Time is precious for everybody, but when you are a celebrity like Snoop, your time becomes even more valuable because you have less of it for yourself. People are just making so many demands and you have so many commitments that you really relish those little moments alone or with your family. I had just stolen about an hour from his life. Not good.

Kevin, whom I love, is from Canada and is about the whitest man I've ever met, which I have no issue with. The problem is, when he gets frustrated or upset or laughs hard, his face turns bright red. So when he is in an "oh shit" moment, he turns bright red. He's bright red because he's like, *Snoop's going to be pissed*. He's upset because we just wasted his time. He doesn't have an hour to spare. That's what people need to understand. You see him on TV every day.

I understand.

This shit's got to be shot. So he has to travel all over the world constantly to do all these events, movies and stuff. That's the price of being an iconic American star.

But it's now time to pay the bill.

This is where compromise really comes in handy. I saw that Kevin was going to have to be with him all day and the next day. My shift was over in two hours.

I looked at Kevin. He was looking at me. And he's like, "Fuck."

I just said, "I got this one."

He looked at me and said, "What?"

I turned, walked over to Snoop, and said, "Boss, I fucked up. I wrote the time down wrong. It's on me. It's all my fault. I apologize."

Snoop just said, "Thanks for stepping up. Next time, check the numbers."

I was like, "I'll be on it, boss. Is there anything I can do?"

He said, "No, you're good. I'm going to go chill in my dressing room."

Kevin looked at me. He said, "What did you say?"

I said, "I told him that you fucked up, and that I was going to take you outside and beat you up."

He's like, "Seriously, what the fuck did you say?"

I said, "Seriously? That's what I said. I said, 'It's compromise, baby.'" I let the joke settle then said, "I took the heat. I said it was on me. I said I screwed up the time."

He said, "What happened?

"He told me, 'Don't do it again.' And he thanked me for stepping up."

The funny part about it was, over the course of our time working together, Kevin and I would take turns on being the bad guy or the one who messed up, but we never did it consistently so he could never get mad at one person.

In a work situation, compromise is often how we deal with people. We have to. It's the same thing. Sometimes you've got to leave your shit at the door, hold your tongue, and listen.

When other people talk, when you disagree with people, or you're like, "Oh, I don't like that guy, he's a Democrat," my argument is always, "Have you ever talked to him? Do you know anything about him? You do? Like, do you guys like the same sport? Do you know his favorite food?"

Find common ground and compromise. You mean to tell me how this guy votes is how you're going to judge him as a person? That's your problem. That's your issue.

If you don't have the ability to compromise, you're not going to succeed, not just in the workplace, but in your personal relationships. You're not going to succeed when you meet people and you are judging them based off of one aspect of who they are.

I have friends all over the political spectrum. Most of the time, I don't talk politics with my friends. There's a lot more to life than politics. We are made of many things. Don't be scared to compromise or meet people halfway. Don't be afraid to make adjustments that help the greater good. We have to try harder. Myself included. A lot of the problems we are seeing today come from political extremes on both sides. If more of us worked to the middle and made some compromises, I think the world would be an easier place than it is.

Unfortunately, that's just not the way it is today. Everybody flies off the handle so quickly when they don't agree with somebody. We judge and judge and judge so quickly. Again, I'm guilty but I'm trying to get better. The older I get, the more I learn about that sweet spot—the middle.

'Nuff Said

AI (and I Don't Mean Allen Iverson)

As I sit here writing this book, artificial intelligence, or AI, is one of the hottest topics in the news. I'm sure by the time this book comes out it will still be a hot topic, but things will have changed a lot because that's just the way this thing is going. It's evolving and changing as fast as anything we have ever witnessed. But I think there are certain constants that will still be relevant by the time you read this.

Right now, we are talking about AI in very simple terms. Can it help kids cheat on college papers? Can it write articles for us? This is just the tip of the iceberg. We've seen the robot dogs. We've seen the sex-surrogate-robot females. That's where it's really going. And if it keeps going in this direction, we are pretty much doomed. Because they will be creating things that don't include any of the bullshit. No laziness. No wokeness. No stupidity. Just speed and efficiency, which is the opposite of where the human race is headed right now. There will no longer be human beings working in factories or law enforcement. Judges and lawyers will be created through artificial intelligence. You won't have to worry about a crooked judge anymore. But at the same time, you won't be able to get a judge to have empathy and understand that maybe somebody was trying to feed their family when they committed the crime. That won't compute. You robbed a bank, you get this sentence. End of story. There will be no more plea bargains or any of that stuff. It will just be very matter-of-fact, cut and dry.

You will also have this problem where you have a surplus of human beings with nothing to do. That puts us into this Terminator-type scenario where AI may decide that we have too many humans, so let's just keep the effective ones and get rid of the rest. That will mean the end of civilization as we know it because we will have billions of human beings laying around doing nothing. Once AI works its way into a position of power and can literally outthink human beings, then it will look at human beings just like they will anything else. Is it efficient? Do we need them? Do we want them? They are eating up the planet. They're taking up too much space.

At that point, what will artificial intelligence decide to do? Cut costs. Cut waste. We'll be viewed as waste. And when human beings become nothing more than waste, we have a big problem. So I would say right now that it would behoove you to become as successful as possible. Get those revenue streams together. Be the best you. If you're not, they might replace you, and it won't be based on color, sex, or feelings. It will be based on whether you are necessary. If you're not, you will be deleted.

Now, don't get me wrong, I'm all for technology and progress. But let's be real. AI is a double-edged sword, and we need to be careful before we go too far down this rabbit hole.

AI has the potential to be incredibly powerful and disruptive. We're already seeing the effects of automation on jobs and the economy, and that's just the beginning. As AI becomes more advanced, it could lead to mass unemployment, inequality, and social unrest. Are we ready for that? I'm not. Probably why you'll find me out on a ranch in Montana with everything I need to live out the rest of my life with my family. Hit me up. We'll talk about the good old days when human beings actually mattered.

Nuff said.

CHAPTER 4

International Pronouns Day

I wrote this the day after international pronouns day. What? You didn't know about international pronouns day? Some background:

International Pronouns Day is an annual event that seeks to make sharing and respecting people's pronouns commonplace. It takes place each year on the third Wednesday of October. The first iteration was on October 17, 2018, and there were participants from 25 countries in every continent except Antarctica. The event was founded by Shige Sakurai with assistance from Genny Beemyn. Gender pronouns are far from new. We use them on a regular basis to both identify and refer to somebody. Describing somebody as 'he' or 'she', groups of 'they' or 'them' alongside referring to inanimate things as 'it' is something many will be very familiar with, but this is only really the beginning of an even more complex language, understanding and acceptance.

International Pronouns Day happens each year on the third Wednesday of October. Referring to people by the pronouns they determine for themselves is basic to human dignity. International Pronouns Day seeks to make respecting, sharing, and educating about personal pronouns commonplace. Print out this selfie sign (or edit it into your pictures), fill in your pronouns, and post on social media using the hashtags #MyPronounsAre and #ShareYourPronouns to tell the world why it's important to use the correct pronouns for everyone. (University of California, San Francisco)

Here's how the University of Illinois at Chicago covered it:

October 11, 2022

The Chancellor's Committee for the Status of LGBTQ+ People celebrates International Pronouns Day Wednesday, Oct. 19. International Pronouns Day began in 2018. Its purpose is to make asking, sharing and respecting personal pronouns commonplace.

Referring to people by the name and pronouns they determine for themselves is a basic human dignity. Using someone's correct pronouns is a way to respect them and create an inclusive environment, just as using a person's name can be a way to respect them. Just as it can be offensive or harassing to make up a nickname for someone and call them that nickname against their will, it can be offensive or harassing to assume someone's pronouns and refer to them using those pronouns if that is not how that person wants to be known.

Actively choosing to ignore the pronouns someone has stated that they go by could imply the oppressive notion that intersex, transgender, nonbinary and gender nonconforming people do not or should not exist. Acknowledging someone's correct pronouns contributes to that person's well-being by reducing harm and further trauma. Our committee reinforces our commitment to greater inclusion of LGBTQ+ folx at UIC with the following resources:

- *Update your preferred name and personal pronouns in Banner and on Zoom.*

  o *We know that pronouns can change, and UIC community members are welcome to update as needed.*

- *UIC Gender and Sexuality Center.*

  o *All-Gender Restrooms.*

- *UIC Bias Reporting Tool: Bias Reporting and Prevention.*

- *For allies: Navigating Allyship.*

- *For faculty:*

  o *Make use of engaged teaching strategies to foster interaction with students.*

  o *Ask your students what they'd prefer to be called and make a note on your roster.*

  o *Coming soon: Center for the Advancement of Teaching Excellence Pronoun Usage.*

That last one really gets me: "Coming soon: Center for the Advancement of Teaching Excellence Pronoun Usage." There will be an entire center for this stuff. Gee, what could go wrong with that?

How did it get to this point? Just how have we allowed "woke" culture to normalize nonsense like this? I think you have to go back to when we started giving out participation awards in youth sports just so every kid would feel like they had accomplished something. Whether they did or not. No, I'm not using the word "they" to represent a specific gender. It's just an informal way of referring to both boys and girls. Yes, boys and girls. That's what you find in schools. Boys. And girls. That's it.

The beginning of participation awards in many ways represents the end of pure competition and success. When the woke started deciding that it wasn't okay to lose and that everybody gets to share in a victory no matter what, they began paving the road toward weakness and victimhood.

No longer was there a need to succeed or be revered or feared. If you take away competition and success, then no one challenges you. And when everyone is a victim, then everyone gets their turn at being special.

My opinion? (And I don't mind offering it because if you're holding this book right now chances are you are at least a little bit curious.) I think we are seeing a direct attack both on capitalism and alpha males. The United States is built upon a system of recognition that if you work hard, apply yourself, and do the right things, odds are good you will succeed. That has always been the model for success. But it's more than just under attack these days. The woke contingent is trying to annihilate that entire concept. Speaking as an alpha male, which is what I consider myself, it's easy to see just how systematic the dismantling of my archetype is. I'm big and I'm bad and I get stuff done. And they can't handle that. When I screw up, I take responsibility and I don't expect awards. They don't like that either. It's all about getting attention for being a victim.

For those of us who don't believe in claiming success that is built upon the backs of other people, we are in trouble. When you play the victim, you no longer have to accept responsibility. It's a very convenient situation. Again, by stripping away the competitive nature, we are diluting and attacking the very fabric of what makes the United States so special.

I can move fast. In my house, I'm the fastest person there is. But outside my house, there are people much faster than me. But, if I identify as a non-binary slug, then you can't compare me to other people. And if you don't recognize me as being the fastest non-binary slug, then you are racist because you are not willing to embrace my fantasy, and that's really the essence of what pronouns are about. They are aspirational fantasies. You want to be something else, so you invent something else and, all of a sudden, everybody has to fall in line and tell you how great you are for being something else. Problem is, you can't just be that something else.

I am so damn tired of the pronoun conversation. It's like every time I turn around, there's some new rule or expectation about what pronouns we're supposed to use for people. I mean, seriously, how many pronouns are we supposed to keep track of? It used to be pretty simple: he, she, and they. But now we've got all these new pronouns like xe, ze, and zir. And don't even get me started on the singular "they"—I mean, I know it's been around for centuries, but now we're supposed to use it all the time? It's like the English language has turned into a minefield.

And let's be real, it's not just the pronouns themselves that are exhausting, it's the constant policing of language. It's like we're all supposed to be walking around with a clipboard, making sure we don't offend anyone with our words. And if we slip up and use the wrong pronoun, we're immediately labeled as a bigot or transphobe. It's like we're all living in some Orwellian nightmare where our every word is scrutinized.

But here's the thing: language is messy. It's always evolving, and there are always going to be disagreements about what words mean and how they should be used. And that's okay! We don't need to have a perfect set of pronouns that work for every single person in every single situation. We just need to be respectful and understanding of each other.

Honestly, sometimes it feels like the pronoun conversation is just a distraction from more important issues. You think that China, Russia, and other world powers for sitting around worrying about pronouns? Of course not. They're planning on how they are going to try and take over the world. And laughing their asses off at us, no doubt. The ridiculousness that is the war over proper pronouns speaks to an arrogant, narcissistic, delusional behavior. It's the result of somebody thinking that their Facebook page is a lot bigger than they think it is. This idea that people are obsessing over you. When in truth, most people don't give a shit. We had pronouns when I was growing up. We called them "nicknames." Nicknames were fine. Nicknames were cool. But you never got pissed off if somebody didn't call you by your nickname. Today, I tell someone my nickname is Big Sexy Tyrus and they say, "You know what? I don't want to call you big sexy Tyrus. I'm just going to call you Tyrus." Then that's what they choose to call me because that's their choice and that's fine by me. We hear about people today who get triggered because the wrong pronouns are used. Think about that for a second. Think about how lucky that person is when the biggest problem in their life is when somebody uses the wrong pronoun or refuses to acknowledge the pronoun they are demanding. It is becoming ridiculous. People are seeking psychotherapy because of pronouns. People are ending friendships because of pronouns. People are losing jobs because of pronouns. This is what we worry about today? Seriously?

When I was a kid, I wanted to be Godzilla. When I would play in the swimming pool, I pretended I was breathing fire and causing tidal waves. I would climb to the top of the steps of the pool, roar from the top of my lungs, and challenge any of my friends to be King Kong and come compete against me. Yes, I identified as Godzilla. The problem was, when I went back home, bursting through the door as Godzilla, my mother sternly brought me back to the reality of who I really was: her punk-ass kid who needed to do his chores. In my mind it was all, "Godzilla doesn't do chores. I'm a fire-breathing beast." But what was in my mind did not matter. Because I did not run that house. My mother did. And so it was time to sweep the kitchen floor, make my bed, and do whatever else she wanted me to do. My mother chose not to invest in my fantasy. Not that she didn't like me playing around like a little boy, but there was a time and a place for everything. In the pool, it was okay to play Godzilla. But at home, there was work that needed to be done and there was no getting around that.

Back then, I guess Godzilla would have been my pronoun. However, my mother, my teachers, and other people in the

neighborhood would not have indulged in my fantasy iden-
tification. So, by today's standards, they are all not just evil
and mean, but also probably racist, homophobic, and misan-
thropic. You can keep adding to the list. That's the way it goes.
You don't respect someone's pronoun? You are the worst kind
of hater. End of story.

I know it sounds ridiculous, but that's the reality today.
What you want to be is not necessarily what you are. You can
aspire to something, and you can work hard to get there, and
if you are lucky and you put the time in, it can happen for you.
But there are some things that can't be changed simply by
willful desires and dreams or proclamations on social media.

I think a lot of people get confused today. They forget that
we are talking about two basic things when it comes to this
issue. Sex, and gender. Look, science is science. 99.99 percent
of your cells have either male or female markings, so you are
a male or female and that's it. You may feel like a woman if
you were born as a man. And you may want to get surgery to
look like a woman, but that does not change your sex. That's
the problem. People want their gender to be treated as a fact,
but you can't just dismiss science. Bears and lions and other
animals in the kingdom don't have a choice, and neither do
we. Pushing gender beliefs on people is like pushing religious
beliefs. You can't make somebody feel what you feel nor can
you demand it and punish them if they don't agree with you.

If you chastise somebody who doesn't know you for assu-
ming you are a he or a she and you begin making speeches to
them about what you identify as, maybe you need to take a
step back. Maybe you're having issues that need to be dealt
with. Maybe you are the one that is being intolerant. Today,
people are taking seven thousand selfies, they are the direc-

tors of their own movies, which has led to so much self-importance and arrogance that we are on the verge of losing control. If someone refers to you as a girl because you clearly look like a girl and act like a girl and you take their head off because you identify as a boy, whose problem is that?

Things like international pronoun day are not helping anything, they are hurting things. They are enabling this mass delusion and anti-science obsession with trying to create a new reality. Just like me thinking I'm Godzilla.

There's a lot of truth to the expression "go woke go broke" when it comes to things like public companies, private companies, and well-known personalities embracing woke culture. When they begin embracing these ridiculous practices like international pronoun day, the majority of the public oftentimes reacts in a negative way that's costing businesses money and celebrities their reputations. The beautiful thing about living in America is, you have a right to identify as Tyrannosaurus Rex, but I have a right to not see you that way myself. As a parent, when your child exhibits this kind of behavior, that's the time to step in and explain to them the true ways of the world. Just like my mother did when I was busy being Godzilla. The pandemic certainly did not help. It forced a lot of people to spend more time alone with their computers and phones exploring what they want to be or worse, what they feel they deserve to be.

I believe that contributed to this mania. Along with contributing to the concept of feeling more special than you are and demanding attention that you have done nothing to deserve.

My first commercial audition back when I was about twenty years old was for McDonald's cheeseburgers. Talk about typecasting. Nobody knew their way around a cheeseburger better than me. This was mine to lose. I thought to myself going into this audition, *I am going to be so good that Ronald McDonald himself is going to emerge from the wings, embrace me, and lead me to the golden arches himself.* When the casting director said, "Action!" I took a big bite of the cheeseburger, smiled, and said "This is delicious." I was killing it. There was nobody out there that was going to outdo my burger bite. I didn't hear from anybody the next day. Not a problem. They probably had to go through the formality of auditioning a lot of people before handing me the gig. After several days, I called the casting number to ask what was going on with the commercial, and they told me it had already been cast. I didn't even get a call back. Again, I was a master cheeseburger eater, so this made no sense to me. How could they not want me? I identified as a cheeseburger eater, for crying out loud. Why was I being deprived of what was naturally and rightfully mine?

Soon after, there was another commercial audition for a football player. Okay. At that time, I was a college football player. A really good football player. I was more of a football player than I was a cheeseburger eater. I was confident I could just go in there, do the audition, and they would hand me the role on the spot.

I went in there, did what I thought was a great audition, and waited for the call. It never came. Now, this was getting weird. It couldn't be that I wasn't doing everything right, because, in my mind, I had decided that I was perfect. It had to be something else. Racism? Hey, why not?

My acting teacher in college liked me. Right around this time, after I performed a monologue, he pulled me aside and said, "I think you are pretty funny, and your timing is decent.

I know you are also a football player, and you should know that it's going to be hard for you to try and succeed both as a football player and as an actor, but, that said, I have something that's a longshot but that I think you might be right for you." My acting teacher was aware of an audition for an upcoming movie called *Saving Private Ryan*. There was a small role that he thought might be good for me, so we shot a short audition tape with me saying a few lines. He told me there were no promises but that he would send it off to Los Angeles. He had explained to me that it was a Tom Hanks movie, and I thought, *This is it. Forget cheeseburgers. I'm on my way. This is my ticket.* He received wor back that casting actually liked my audition, and that was all I needed to know. I was ready to punch my ticket not just for Hollywood but for the Academy Awards. I had been working in the kitchen of a local restaurant, but I quit because hey, I was going to be working not just with Tom Hanks but also with Steven Spielberg. I was no longer going to be any kind of nine-to-five worker. In my drama class, I started separating myself because now I felt special. I was a method actor and couldn't be mingling with all of the other pedestrians in class. I needed my own special space. This was all about me.

And I broke up with my girlfriend. I didn't need that personal baggage when I would be leaving for Italy to start shooting some World War II scenes. My drama teacher had explained to me that would be the location. This was getting exciting. At least in my mind. I recruited a buddy to "manage" my upcoming Hollywood career because Lord knew things were about to start getting crazy. I began to get concerned about production dates and how they would coincide with my football schedule so I went to ask my teacher about how the calendar would shake out. That's when he told me that Spielberg had gone with someone else. I had my Academy Awards speech all written. I had quit my job and basically alienated everyone around me. By the way, the actor who got that small role was Vin Diesel. When I finally saw the movie I tore him apart, I couldn't believe he had gotten the role over me. This was a guy I had never met in my life and yet I wished bad things upon him for taking away what I was rightfully owed. Had Twitter existed back then I would've been all over it trashing him.

I had identified as a cheeseburger eater, as a football player, and as a soldier in a big Hollywood movie. I had decided that's what it was. But none of those things happened. Looking back, obviously I wasn't right for those things. No matter what I thought. Because it's not always about what you think. It's about what others think. That's the point of the story. You can think and dream and want to do great things, that's wonderful, but that doesn't mean you get to automatically claim them. You have to put the time in. And...sometimes you have to be a little lucky. That's just life.

So don't look for me to be celebrating international pronouns day anytime soon. We are what we are. We can try and be what we want to be, but there are no guarantees.

𝔑𝔲𝔣𝔣 𝔖𝔞𝔦𝔡

The Boys Have No Business Playing with the Girls

We need to have a real talk about something that's been bugging me for a while now. I'm talking about the issue of biological males competing in women's sports. Let's get something straight: it's not fair, it's not right, and it's not okay.

Now, I know there are those out there who will argue that gender identity is more important than biological sex, and that if someone identifies as a woman, they should be able to compete in women's sports. But here's the thing: biological sex is a scientific fact, not a social construct. And when it comes to sports, there are physical differences between males and females that cannot be ignored.

Let me break it down for you. On average, biological males have greater muscle mass, larger bone structure, and higher levels of testosterone than biological females. This gives them a clear physical advantage in sports that rely on strength, speed, and power. And it's not just about the numbers, it's about the way the male body is structured and how it responds to training.

I'm not saying that biological males should be banned from sports altogether. Far from it. But when it comes to competitive sports, there needs to be a level playing field.

I can hear the argument already: "But what about trans women who have undergone hormone therapy? They don't have an unfair advantage!" Here's the thing, even with hormone therapy, biological males still have physical advantages over biological females. Also, hormone therapy can take years to have a significant impact on muscle mass and other physical factors.

Keep in mind the impact this has on biological female athletes. When they have to compete against biological males, they're at a disadvantage. They're competing against athletes who have a clear physical advantage, and that can be demoralizing and unfair. It can also have a negative impact on their chances of getting scholarships, sponsorships, and other opportunities in sports.

I know there are those out there who will argue that this is discriminatory or unfair to trans athletes. But let me be clear: this is not about discrimination. It's about creating a level playing field for all athletes, regardless of their gender identity or biological sex. Trans athletes should be able to compete in sports, just like anyone else. But when it comes to competitive sports, we need to take into account the physical realities of biological sex.

Biological male athletes invading women's sports to compete with the obvious knowledge that they have a better chance of being successful is the most misogynistic, "toxic masculinity" thing a man could do. Period.

It needs to stop. Here's the deal. Sports is discriminating by definition. You are being assessed based solely on your ability to successfully play the sport. If there are nine spots on a basketball team and there's ten players and nine of them are far superior, the tenth person is not making the team. No one's going to say, "Well, they're so nice and need to be on the team." No one cares. Because it's sports. You are judged on your performance.

When you see male athletes that have participated most of their lives as men, then they get to a certain place and decide to "become" a woman and compete against women, it's unfair. It's bullshit. Lia Thomas, for example, was ranked 200 in men's swimming, switched over to the women's and boom, dominated. All of a sudden. Lia is winning every swim event, in some cases by ridiculous record-breaking numbers. Why justify this? Why let feelings get in the way? Feelings are irrelevant when it comes to sports, feelings should be irrelevant, period. Because they're feelings. They're not facts. Your feelings. My feelings. Everyone has them. It's like elbows. Everyone's got at least two. Doesn't make them law. And no one else has to acknowledge your feelings. So there's no place for biological men in women sports at all.

When you have somebody who is an Olympic Gold medalist and one of the greatest athletes of the twentieth century, Caitlyn Jenner, who has transitioned to living her life as a woman, when she is the first one to come out and say at no point should this be tolerated, then I stand with her. She has been so intellectually honest and upfront about all of this. and I've had the privilege of talking about this with her firsthand and she walks it like she talks it. The real deal. Somebody that we should listen to. As she says, she never would've done this.

She understands the ridiculously unfair advantage that she would've had competing against other women.

You want to transition? Be my guest. But as soon as you decide to step into the realm of sports, your feelings don't mean fuck all. It comes down to raw data and stats. A basketball player might want to identify as a guy who scores forty points a game, but if he only scores ten, guess what? We're not going to change his stats because he wants to identify as a guy who scored forty. Biological men competing in women's sports is the same thing. If a man who transitioned to a woman decided to compete with men and win, wouldn't that be a bigger victory for trans women? But we won't see that. Because many of these athletes failed in the male category and they know that they can now achieve their dreams by competing against people that, by nature, they are stronger than. It's one big scam. So the answer is no. There's no place for biological men in women sports in any situation. Anyone who says differently is being paid by or being sponsored by the LBGTQ community that's pushing this. No unfair advantages should be tolerated. That's why people like Barry Bonds and Roger Clemens will probably never wind up in the Hall of Fame. Because it is believed that they used human growth hormones and steroids to give themselves unfair advantages. It's the same with biological men competing in women's sports.

I hope this corrects itself soon. I hope women's groups stand strong and fight against us. And I hope all of these people who claim to be for women's rights but support this kind of ridiculousness wake up to their own hypocrisy and realize that when you support biological men competing against biological women in organized sports, you are doing women a massive injustice.

Why not just create a nonbinary category? Let them have their own division. Let them organize it, let them fund it, let them make it real. See if it can succeed. Let the market dictate whether or not there is interest in non-binary competitions. That will take care of it. In the meantime, memo to biological male athletes that now claim they are women, leave the real women to their own competitions. You have no place in there.

Nuff said.

CHAPTER 5

Sea Turtles

As you may know, if you follow me at all, I have a real thing about reptiles and amphibians, particularly fish, but pretty much any creature that has fins, scales, likes to slither, or lives in the water. I'm not sure why. Maybe it's because all of them, for the most part, move silently through life. They are stealthy. I may be known for being vocal on many topics, but my core being is way more in tune with those creatures. I'm quiet. I move through the jungle as silently as I can, always observing, always looking out for the things I care about, be it my beloved children, or simply my ideas about life.

I wish I could raise sea turtles. I doubt that will ever happen. They are a very protected species, highly sensitive, and not the sort of thing it would be smart to try and keep in your house no matter how elaborate an aquarium system you might have. But I have an emotional attachment to sea turtles, especially the mothers. I will get to that in a bit.

For now, I'm just going to put it straight. Sometimes, the best relationship is no relationship at all. They say blood is thicker than water, but I think that depends on how deep the scars are. When it comes to my mother, we don't have what most people would consider any kind of relationship. We don't see each other. We don't talk to each other. We don't write to each other. But it's not like I don't think about her. And when I think about sea turtles, I think about my mom....

My mother and I went through lots of trauma together when I was a little boy living in that cramped Boston-area apartment I wrote about in my first book. There were several incidents that I didn't write about, but, since then, I've thought long and hard about what I feel I need to share with you. And I'm finally ready to talk about one incident in particular that changed my life for better and worse.

My brother and I witnessed what my mother went through with my real dad on a daily basis. Thinking back on it, it was even more nightmarish than my seven-year-old brain could have ever hoped to process. One thing I clearly remember about the situation was, the innocents never get a break. The moments of calm between the brutality are reserved for the abuser. Because everybody else is waiting for the next round of hell to begin. Everyone else is worried about saying or doing the wrong thing.

Especially my mother.

She was constantly on eggshells, anxious about what would trigger him next, while simultaneously trying to create a normal life for her two sons: cleaning us, feeding us, and constantly reassuring us that everything was going to be okay. I can't imagine what it was like for her to lie to her children every night as she tucked us in, pretending that somehow there was a way out of everything that was happening. She knew there wasn't, but she wanted us to believe there was.

She knew that he was always one drink or one line of cocaine away from losing his mind and slapping her around. With that in her mind, she also, somehow, worked hard at trying to fulfill all of his needs.

I'm an alpha male. In my entire life, I've never been in physical fear because of another person. I may not like them, but it never matters. There's no way anybody else has ever been able to slam a door shut, lock it in front of me, and then say, "Your ass ain't going nowhere." Trust me, my big ass can always leave, and there's nothing anybody on this planet can do about it. So, there has never been a way for me to relate to what my mom was going through. I could sympathize, but I couldn't empathize. As a male, I knew damn well that, because I also had my father's DNA, I had the capability of behaving like him at some point down the line. I didn't want to think about that, but it was reality. We are what we are. With my mother's DNA, however, there was no way physically I would ever be in a position like she was. It just was not possible.

As I learned, and as I know she was all too well aware of, sometimes the fear of the unknown is worse than the unknown itself. Because the unknown manifests itself in your mind; it spins out of control exponentially and morphs into every worst nightmare you have ever feared. The unknown becomes a chamber of midnight madness. It forces you to consider many brutal options that may or may not happen. My mom lived in fear of the known, as well as the unknown.

My father's paranoid obsession was that my mother was cheating on him. Keep in mind that not only was she not cheating on him, but he cheated on her whenever he felt like it. And he felt like it a lot. I'm sure the drugs he was doing contributed to his insecure delusions, but it didn't change anything. He was convinced she was unfaithful.

I've never shared publicly what I'm about to tell you now, and while it's not easy for me to write about, I feel it's important to tell you the story because it taught me something not just about my mom, but all mothers trapped in abusive situations.

My father came home one night convinced my mother was sleeping with a guy who lived a floor above us. I was hiding in my bedroom and could hear him calling her every name in the book. There was a pause in his verbal attack when I heard footsteps approaching my closed bedroom door. It opened abruptly, startling me. "Get out here now," he said coldly.

I slowly walked out into the small living space and could see my mom sobbing on the couch. The side of her face was bright red from where he had slapped her. I wasn't sure what he wanted from me, but after a minute or so, he made it clear. Kneeling down next to me, I was hit with all of the terrible scents that I associated with him over the years—the cheap rotten whiskey on his breath, the stale sweat, the cocoa butter he mixed into his hair with Vaseline. I could feel his warm breath against the side of my face when he slurred, "Tell your mom she is a whore."

I had heard him call her that on numerous occasions, but there was no way I was going to call her that. I remained silent. I didn't react.

"Say it," he hissed. "Call your mom a dirty whore. Say the words, 'Mommy is a dirty whore.'"

At that point, my eyes locked with my mother's eyes. I will never forget that moment because, without saying a word, I could feel her imploring me to do what I needed to save myself. Her knowing eyes were saying to me, "It's okay, George. They are just words. Say them, because if you don't, he's going to hurt you." Tears were forming in her eyes. I understood.

"Mommy is a whore," I whispered.

"Louder," he directed me.

"Mommy is a whore...Mommy's a whore...Mommy is a whore...."

My mom and I never stopped looking at each other. She was giving me a look only a mother can do. Now we both had tears in our eyes.

My father wasn't done. "And what happens to dirty whores? Tell me what happens to dirty whores!"

I didn't know the answer. I had no idea what to do. I thought for sure there was a blow coming for my head, but instead, he kept talking.

"Dirty whores get beat. You smack a dirty whore. They are trash. They ain't worth shit."

There was a bleak silence for several moments until he continued.

"Now, you better tell me. Have you ever seen another man in this house? Has mommy ever left you to go to another man's house? You better not lie to me."

After I numbly shook my head, "No," he ordered me back to my bedroom, but I could still hear what was going on out there.

My mother was pleading quietly, "I would never hurt you. I love you. I am loyal to you."

Why she felt the need to satisfy his every whim I will never understand. Abusive relationships are complex and sometimes beyond understanding. It just was what it was. In my opinion, my mother was a long-term rape victim. When a woman has sex with you out of fear of being beaten, you can call it whatever you want, but to me, it is rape. Doing something to avoid getting an ass-whooping? No question in my mind.

Lying in bed that night, I was too scared to go to the bathroom, so I wet myself. This began a bad habit of me being scared to go to the bathroom when hell was breaking loose on the outside, so I would end up soiling myself and then flushing my underwear down the toilet. This backfired on me, literally, one night soon after when I flushed all my clothes, corduroy pants and all, down the toilet and backed up the entire apartment building's plumbing system. The superintendent had to come up and pull all of my clothes out of the piping, and while my mother was upset about it, my father just laughed it off.

For five years, this brutal cycle of abuse continued. My mother continued to protect me and my younger brother, but, somehow, I knew she would never be the same after all this. How could she be? As I wrote in *Just Tyrus*, she gave us up for several years so she could get a nursing degree, which, in her view, would help make our lives better. But what I didn't write about the first time around is what happened when we were reunited. When she saw my face, I could tell things would never be the same with us again. I looked exactly like a lighter-skinned version of my father. Same smile, same nose, same brow, same everything. All of a sudden, she was staring into the face of the monster who for years had been hell-bent on destroying her. When you see that face, subconsciously you are going to feel a certain way. I don't think she could ever get past it.

I will never hold any ill will against my mother for not being able to fully connect with me once I took on the physical appearance of my father. When she gave us up during that time, it made us tough, but it also allowed us to experience what it was like to have a real father. The couple that fostered us were sensitive, caring, and responsible people who taught us many valuable lessons and provided us with a sense of normalcy. I rely on those memories every day as I continue to develop my own fatherhood skills, and I never would have learned those lessons had she not given us up.

We tried so many times over the years to make it right, but it always came down to the same thing. Too much baggage. We've been through too much together. It just never seems to work. A lot of the old pain comes up and, as much as we try to make sense of it, everything implodes. But, trust me, we have tried. Things feel good for a moment and then, all of a sudden, they spiral.

From what I understand, my mom has a good life. She's happy. She paid her dues and deserves everything she has. I don't monitor her or keep tabs because that's not what letting go is all about. When you let someone go, you have to truly let them go or it becomes impossible to move on. If the baggage doesn't allow you to move forward together, then you have to move forward apart. There's just too much pain in our past, and I accept that.

Sometimes, the hardest thing to do is to let go of what you love the most. But you do it for the higher good.

Now, about those sea turtles... If you don't know about sea turtle mothers, they will travel the world until they find the perfect beach with the perfect sand, the perfect temperature, the perfect moisture, the perfect environment. Then she crawls out onto a difficult terrain she's not built to walk upon. But she does it. Then she digs a hole deep enough to keep predators away from her precious eggs. Then she covers them up with sand. She has set them up for success. Exhausted, she drags herself back into the water. She will never see what happens to them. But she's given them their best chance at a good life.

My mother did what she had to do to give us the best chance at a good life. Mom, I don't know if you're reading this right now, but I want to tell you directly, from me to you, from your little boy who, a long time ago, looked deep into your eyes during one of the most painful moments in our lives, and learned firsthand what it means to be a mother: Thank you. For doing what you did so that I had a chance. For keeping me safe. For walking through hell for me. Maybe we can't come together to be a family, but whenever things get tough in my life, I think about you and what you did for me. Your sacrifices will always keep me going.

I love you, Mom.

No matter what.

'Nuff Said

Leave Animals Alone

We need to have a little chat about something that's been grinding my gears. I'm talking about all you fools out there who think it's a good idea to confront wildlife in order to snap a quick selfie or harass the poor critters. Let me tell you something, this behavior is not only stupid, it's downright dangerous.

First of all, let's get one thing straight: wild animals are just that—wild. They don't care about your Instagram feed, or your Facebook likes, or your TikTok followers. They have their own lives to live and their own rules to follow, and if you get in their way, you're likely to get hurt.

Think about it. Would you go up to a grizzly bear or a mountain lion and try to take a selfie with it? Of course not! You'd be risking your life. And yet, people seem to think it's perfectly fine to harass smaller animals like squirrels, raccoons, and birds.

Newsflash, people: these animals are not your playthings. When you confront them, you're not only putting yourself in danger, you're also disrupting their natural behavior.

And let's not forget about the impact this behavior can have on the environment. When people start feeding wildlife or leaving garbage around, animals become dependent on humans for food and lose their ability to forage for themselves. This can lead to overpopulation and other problems, which can have a ripple effect throughout the ecosystem.

But let's get back to the issue at hand: why are people so obsessed with taking selfies with animals in the first place? Is it really worth risking your safety and the safety of the animals just to get a few likes on social media?

Part of the problem is that people have become disconnected from nature. We spend so much time indoors, staring at screens, that we've forgotten what it's like to be outside experiencing the natural world. So, when come across wild animals, we feel the need to capture the moment and share it with the world. But here's the thing: you don't need to take a selfie with a wild animal in order to appreciate it. In fact, you're better off just observing from a safe distance and letting the animal go about its business. You'll still be able to appreciate its beauty and wildness without putting yourself or the animal in danger.

So, what can we do to combat this behavior? For starters, we need to educate people about the dangers of confronting wildlife. We need to make it clear that this behavior is not only stupid, but, in many cases, it's illegal. Parks and other protected areas should have signs and other educational materials that explain why it's important to leave wildlife alone and how to safely observe from a distance.

We also need to hold people accountable when they engage in this behavior. If you see someone harassing wildlife, speak up. Report them to park rangers or other authorities. And if you're with someone who wants to take a selfie with a wild animal, don't be afraid to speak up and tell them why it's a bad idea, why they should channel that impulse into reconnecting with nature to appreciate the beauty and value of wildlife in its natural habitat.

The next time you're out in nature and come across a wild animal, resist the urge to get too close or snap a quick selfie. Instead, take a moment to appreciate the wonder of the natural world and let the animals go about their business in peace. Trust me, your social media followers will survive, and the animals will be better off for it.

I don't come at this lightly. I've been an animal person my entire life. Next to my family, the most important thing to me right now is my tropical fish collection. The amount of care and time and energy I've put into those creatures has taught me a lot about life and continues to do so. Responsibility, respect: there are many things that I learn from tending to my many fish in dozens of aquariums. It's a process. They live or die based on my behavior. I'm not in there taking selfies with them. I'm feeding them and keeping their tanks clean. And taking care of whatever else they need. I get this.

If you see a buffalo at Yellowstone Park, don't walk up and pet it. Don't go pet the baby bears. You're going to get your ass chewed up. Worst of all, you're going to get them shot and murdered. Again, I take this seriously. I always have and I always will. David Attenborough is one of my favorite human beings on the planet. Sir David. I don't think I've missed one episode of anything he's narrated. My dream at one point in my life was to be a zoologist, but the work in the labs conflicted with football and acting. Still, I've never stopped studying animals. I've never stopped thinking about our relationship with nature.

Nature is beautiful. It's one of the best parts of life, and you can enjoy it anytime. Go find a park. Stop and sit down and just stare at some flowers. All of a sudden, you'll see a bee, then you'll see a spider somewhere, or a fly, maybe a little lizard coming up doing its thing. Mother Nature is beautiful. It's the best way to relax and think. I enjoy observing nature and being a part of it.

I'm a conservationist at heart. I believe that if you see something cool in nature, let it be. If you've got a lizard on your wall, don't catch him and put him in a tank. Just watch. Enjoy him. I've had a lizard living in my front yard for the longest time. I see him every day, I acknowledge him when I walk by. "Morning, bro." He's just out there doing his thing. We are part of nature. Let's act like it. Let's protect it.

Nuff said.

CHAPTER 6

The Court of Twitter

I like what Elon Musk is doing as of this writing, but he still has a long way to go when it comes to Twitter.

"The court of Twitter" is a phrase that has gained popularity in recent years, particularly in the context of social media and online culture. At its core, the term refers to the idea that Twitter has become a platform where individuals can express their opinions and judgments on various issues and events, and where these opinions can carry significant weight in shaping public discourse.

The concept is rooted in the idea that Twitter has given rise to a new kind of public sphere, one in which individuals can engage in public debate and discourse in a way that was not possible before. In the past, public debate was largely limited to traditional media outlets like newspapers, television, and radio, which were controlled by a small number of gatekeepers. Social media, however, has democratized access to public discourse, allowing anyone with an internet connection to voice their opinions and engage with others.

While this democratization of conversation has many benefits, it has also given rise to new challenges and risks. One of the most significant risks is the potential for online harassment and the spread of misinformation. In the court of Twitter, individuals can be publicly shamed and called out for perceived wrongdoings, often without a fair trial or due process. This can lead to serious consequences, really bad things like a ruined reputation, loss of income, and even legal action in some cases.

Another risk of the court of Twitter is the potential for groupthink and the echo chamber effect. Because social media algorithms are designed to show users content that is similar to what they have already engaged with, it is easy for individuals to become trapped in a bubble of like-minded opinions and perspectives. This can lead to a lack of diversity in public discourse and a narrowing of the range of opinions and perspectives that are considered valid.

Despite these risks, the court of Twitter also has many benefits. One of the best things is how social media helps facilitate the democratization of public discourse. By allowing anyone with an internet connection to voice their opinions and engage with others, social media has opened up new avenues for public debate and discussion. This can help to promote democratic values like free speech, equal representation, and the free exchange of ideas.

In addition, the court of Twitter can be a powerful tool for holding individuals and organizations accountable. By exposing unethical practices and calling out offensive behavior, Twitter users can help to promote true social justice and hold those in power accountable for their actions. This can be particularly important in cases where traditional media outlets are unwilling to report on certain issues.

The court of Twitter also has the potential to facilitate the formation of new communities and the building of social capital. By connecting individuals with shared interests and values, Twitter can help to foster the formation of new social networks and communities. This can be particularly important for marginalized groups who may not have access to traditional social networks and communities.

This is all true, but...the court of Twitter is also a lynch mob. Often, it doesn't care about facts. They try to take down what they fear. And they can't do it in a court of law because that requires facts, not feelings.

This mob is very insecure and they're attention seeking. You can tell because they spend their whole day trying to get strangers to like them. They post pictures of their food and their pets. They take seven thousand selfies, all at different angles with different filters. They need you to look. They're desperate for people to like them. You are of a simple mind if you need attention from people you don't know. It's a delusion of grandeur. They make a Facebook page with an avatar of themselves, and it's the best version of themselves. They post a picture and get twenty likes from people with comments that say, "You look great." Now they seem to think that, and they get called an influencer, but it's a fake star. They think they're movie stars, TV stars, fashion models. They think people watch them, and they write blogs and they have live "hangouts." And you watch them do this shit and you just look at and they don't realize that most people look at them like a reality TV show or the last act at the end of the tent at the carnival where it's the crazy lizard freak with the forked tongue or the skeleton of the nine-foot man. It's an anomaly. You're like, "Oh, my God, look at that." You'll see a two-headed baby calf in a bottle of formaldehyde, the freak show you have to stop and gawk at. That's the average person on social media. People think the two-headed calf in the bottle is this amazing, important person. And they can even buy likes and followers. It's just, "Look at me!" They're like penguins stealing rocks from each other. "I'm important."

With that delusion and those feelings, those first-world problems, they feel they have power over anyone who does anything they don't like. Power over anyone who does something that might hurt their ability to get attention. Or worse, somebody gets more attention than they do. They've got to take them down. So they'll spend their time trying to find something to take them down with. And it is a powerful tool because they don't need facts. They don't need truth. All they need is an allegation and a few other like-minded people to get involved.

And then they virtue signal and use those magic words that someone's racist or sexist or misogynistic. Or my favorite, "toxic masculinity." Of course, masculinity is toxic to anybody who's not accountable. So that's what they do. They travel in packs, they group together, and then they find someone. It's usually somebody vastly more successful than them. They never punch down. They only swing up and they will find something. They'll find a guy who just got drafted by the NHL. He's excited, and they don't like it. They dig up something from when he was twelve years old, something racist he posted on Twitter. They form a coalition to go after him. And then the team folds because they have the illusion that this group of trolls, for lack of a better word, are more powerful than they are because they appear to get "likes." So those in charge say, "You know what? We just make the problem go away because we can get another kid. We draft another kid," and they cut the kid. For youthful ignorance, which everyone has done. And that's the mob. Always looking to take down.

The hilarious thing is that none of these cancelling trolls has ever achieved the fame of the person they've taken out. That's the part I laugh at. For all their work and all their effort, they're still obscure. Because they don't matter. They don't build healthy relationships. They want to live in the fantasy that they're famous. It's a delusion. That's what Twitter and those other social media outlets do.

When do these trolls strive for? Comments. "Is anyone agreeing with me? Does everyone like me? How many likes do I have? Oh, did I get followers?" That is about as sad as a person can possibly get.

If an actor is drunk driving and hits somebody, he gets arrested. He goes to court. The prosecution puts their case together, the defense puts their case together, and the jury makes the decision, and then he gets his consequences. It's fair because it's facts based. Social media is feelings based.

Here's the cool part. The mob that tries to get everything shut down doesn't spend money on products. They don't go to the movies. They barely support anything, if they have any money at all, they put it on getting likes on their social media feeds. They don't affect real industry. There is nothing to fear with these people. They mean nothing. Corporate America, if you are reading this, please note: Don't be scared of the shrill minority. They don't spend money. At least not the money you are worried about.

The average American works and raises their kids. They go out on the weekends if they can. They spend very little time on social media. Those are the people out buying stuff, the people who go to the movies, the people who go on vacations. They work for their livings so they can afford nice things. They don't spend their time trying to get people to like the breakfast that they had, or bash Starbucks because a Karen complained they didn't get her coffee fast enough.

So how do you how do you deal with the Twitter court mob? You don't participate. I won't participate. How do you do that? I have a couple of tips.

One of the things that I always do when somebody comes after me on social media is I take a deep breath, I smirk, and I block them. Now I can't see them. I can't see their tweets. I can't see the shit that they're saying about me. When I step outside, away from my phone or my computer, they're not outside. They're not around. I don't know them. It's like somebody put graffiti on a wall about me.

Now, if you've done something egregious or you've been accused of something on a mass scale and you are a celebrity, then you obviously get a lawyer. But, generally speaking, most of the time when these people go after you, it's small stuff. Do not engage because the engagement is what they're after. They want your acknowledgment because they feel it gives them clout. Essentially, they want to be famous without putting in the work. They want to be known without respect. And they want to be able to pass judgment without wisdom. They just want to do what they want to do based on how they feel.

They went after Dave Chappelle. Netflix said, "No, you don't like it, maybe you shouldn't be here." The world didn't blow up. And Netflix didn't go out of business. Why? Because the people that were calling to cancel Dave Chappelle didn't have enough numbers to affect subscription rates on Netflix. If it wasn't for the CEO at Netflix having a pair and saying, no, maybe this isn't the place for you to work if you don't like our content, they would have taken down one of the biggest comedians in this country and taken him off the air to satisfy what is "best."

We're witnessing a shift. And I'm happy to say by book three, I think we'll see the end. I'm being a little bit of a Nostradamus here, but I think we're going to see the end of cancel culture in the next year because it took a while for the big companies to realize there's no money in it.

Everything changes when the consumer says "enough." And when the consumer says enough, they become the real mob. You know why they're the real mob? Because they're the ones who have the cash. They buy the beer. And when they say enough, we're not buying it anymore, that's it. Bud Light has supposedly lost billions in stock value over going woke with that ad campaign, and you don't think the Dylan dude and those that brought him in are out of favor with Bud Light? They are. Because you just cost money and jobs. That's real consequences.

When I was about twelve, I got an opportunity as a kid to try out for a Pony League baseball team after a coach saw me playing in the street with some friends. This is when kids played outside in neighborhoods, and we used to play baseball in the street with a tennis ball and a bat. This coach saw me hit a tennis ball that disappeared from view. He said, "You should come down and try out." I was like, "Cool." I asked my mom, and she said sure.

The next day, I got dropped off and walked to the top of the park. It was a pretty good walk to the field. When I arrived, I saw that everybody on the team had a mom, dad, or grandparent there, and they all seemed very close. The kids had been playing together on this travel team and had grown up and come up through the system together. Everybody knew everybody, but nobody knew me.

I had a glove that my grandmother gave me for my birthday. I was in a pair of sweats and had my hat on backwards. Pretty much how you see me on TV is how I looked, take away the beard and about a foot and a half of height.

I did not fit in when I got to the field. Parents looked at me. I was different. I think I heard one of the moms, I feel like her name was Karen, say, "He needs to turn his hat around."

I walked over, the coach introduced me to the team and said I was going to be trying out. The kids had no problem with this. Kids don't think bad things about an outsider who looks different unless an adult pushes them to. I was just a big kid with a wooden bat who was trying to help the team. But Karen had a problem with me. I think that was clear to everybody. She was her own little woke mob rolled up into one uptight, stressed-out racist white woman. She was one of those classic Little League moms who thought she ran the show. She clearly did not want me there. I was the only kid of color on that field, and I think that's why she had it in for me. I wanted to play first base, I was getting all ready to take the position until she said something and, all of a sudden, I was moved to the outfield. I was canceled. Had Twitter been around back then I'm sure she would've been blasting me right then and there from her phone. During the practice I noticed my wooden Louisville slugger was in contrast to every other aluminum bat on that field.

She didn't like me, she didn't like my attitude, she liked nothing about me. And she clearly had some power. She wasn't just a troll, she had some clout. So I'm acting like a good soldier, I go out there in the outfield, shagged a bunch of fly balls, and I made some strong throws to the plate. They're not going to slow me down. They think they can cancel me, but they really can't. Then it came time to take a few swings as it was getting dark. Again, I was the last kid in the box to hit. Karen was right behind home plate, smirking and snickering as I took the first pitch because I didn't like it. I was always taught, don't swing at a pitch if you don't like it. She didn't like that. So now I hear her starting a little whisper campaign behind my back in the stands where she had moved to. "What is this kid doing here? He's a troublemaker. He has no place here...I don't think you can even hit the ball...."

Keep talking, Karen. Keep trolling. Now, I'm getting pissed. But I know getting angry isn't going to help my game, so I keep internalizing it. I'm like an angry young Incredible Hulk out there, at least that's what I was feeling like, especially with that Louisville Slugger in my hands. I stepped out of the box and gave her a good long stare. And she knew I was locked in on her. It was like a damn staring contest there, both of us trying to prove our points. I think she was getting as pissed as I was. I was feeding off of that energy. Sometimes the trolls have no idea how they fuel you. A few other pitches came and went. I popped a few up, I hit a couple of grounders, nothing special. And she was feeding off of that. I could hear the snickers getting louder. The next pitch came in, it sat up for me in the zone, and I connected. I felt it off the bat. Sweet spot all the way. I watched the ball launch off of the bat and streak into the night. I called out to the leftfielder, "Don't bother," turned around and said the same thing to her. Don't bother. That thing was long gone, and everybody knew it. I had proven my point. I definitely belonged out there. I was becoming a wise ass, that's one of the first lines I remember delivering in public, and I remember it like it happened five minutes ago.

When people come at me, I come right back at them. I don't blink.

I will admit, I exchanged a few words with her that day and in the days afterward. Coach pulled me aside and told me I couldn't do that, and he was right. I had a lot of learning to do. But she had tried to race me before I even got out of the gate. She did not want me on that field, and she was building a case against me to all the other parents and coaches on that field. And guess what? When everybody saw what I could do, that was all the proof they needed to ignore her. I like seeing companies today that stand by their products, stand by their ideas, stand by their marketing, and don't get intimidated. But when you fold. When you let them taste blood. When you give in. Then the game is over. Then you have no place on the field.

Nuff Said

The Border

Listen up. We've got a problem at our southern border, and it's time to stop beating around the bush and start taking some real action. The situation down there is a mess, and it's only getting worse by the day. We've got illegal immigrants pouring into our country, drugs and weapons being smuggled in left and right, and violent criminals slipping through the cracks. It's time to stop playing politics and start addressing these problems head-on.

Let's start with the illegal immigration crisis. It's no secret that we've got a massive influx of people coming across our border, and it's putting a serious strain on our resources. Our immigration system is already overburdened, and we simply can't handle the number of people trying to come in illegally. This isn't just bad for our country—it's bad for the people who are risking their lives to make the journey.

It's not just a matter of logistics. We have to consider the fact that not everyone who crosses the border is doing so with good intentions. We've seen countless cases of drug smugglers, human traffickers, and violent criminals slipping through the cracks and making their way into our communities. It's not just a matter of securing our borders—it's a matter of protecting our citizens.

So what do we do about it? First, we need to secure our border. That means building a wall, increasing patrols, and investing in technology to monitor and track activity. We also need to crack down on employers who are hiring illegal immigrants, and we need to streamline our immigration process to make it easier for people to come here legally.

But we can't just stop there. We need to address the root causes of illegal immigration. That means working with the governments of Central and South American countries to improve economic opportunities and reduce violence and corruption. We also need to address the demand for drugs in our country and the role it plays in fueling the cartels that are driving so much of the illegal activity at our border.

Speaking of drugs, that brings us to our next problem: drug smuggling. The amount of drugs that are being smuggled across our border is staggering. We're talking about billions of dollars' worth of cocaine, heroin, meth, and fentanyl. And it's not just a matter of people using drugs—it's a matter of the violence and instability that these drugs are causing.

Again, we need to take action. We need to invest in our border patrol and give them the resources they need to combat drug smuggling. We need to work with our international partners to disrupt drug cartels and dismantle their operations. And we need to address the demand for drugs in our country by investing in addiction treatment and prevention programs.

And we need to address the issue of violent criminals coming across our border. This is a serious problem, and it's one that's been ignored for far too long. We're talking about murderers, rapists, and gang members who are slipping through the cracks and posing a serious threat to our communities.

We need to take a hardline stance on this. We need to increase our screening and vetting processes for people coming across our border. We need to work with our international partners to identify and apprehend violent criminals before they make it across our border. And we need to ensure that those who are caught are prosecuted to the fullest extent of the law.

But most importantly, we need to come together as a country and put aside our political differences. This isn't a Republican problem or a Democratic problem—it's an American problem. We need to work together to find solutions that will protect our citizens, secure our border, and uphold the values that make our country great. So let's roll up our sleeves and get to work. The future of our country depends on it.

Many of these people are seeking asylum and they're coming for the American dream. I get it. But there's a right way to come into America and there's a wrong way. And it's not just all at the border. A lot of people get visitor visas or vacation visas, whatever; they fly in on Southwest and they just stay. There are many ways to come into this country. And yeah, we have the current administration telling us none of this is a problem. The gaslighting continues. The rancher in Texas can't sleep at night because he's got anywhere from hundreds to thousands of people coming through his property. And the Biden administration tells him it's not a problem. That they are doing a good job controlling the border. Some people coming through are good people looking for a better life for them and their family. But many are bad. Criminals, pedophiles, drug traffickers; people who are in debt and who will do anything to make money to pay off the drug cartels so their families aren't beheaded. These are real things that are happening on the front line at the border. Personally I think it's become a military thing. Not the National Guard, but serious military enforcement on the border. That's what it's going to take. And I doubt this administration feels the commitment to go in there and get it done. People are tired of living in fear. And they are also tired of seeing illegal immigrants get special treatment, put up in hotels with good food, medical attention, and everything else on the taxpayer dime.

And the so-called sanctuary cities don't even want to act like a sanctuary when illegal immigrants are bussed into their town. Are those political stunts? Maybe. But sometimes you need political stunts to make people pay attention. Bottom line, don't call yourself a sanctuary city if you're not willing to be a haven for whomever arrives at your door. Otherwise it's just more virtue-signaling bullshit that is becoming such a trademark of the left.

Nuff said.

CHAPTER 7

𝕬re 𝖄ou 𝕽ight for the 𝕵ob?

"I am obviously acutely aware that my presence at this podium represents a few firsts. I am a Black, gay, immigrant woman, the first of all three of those to hold this position," she said. "If it were not for generations of barrier-breaking people before me, I would not be here. But I benefit from their sacrifices. I have learned from their excellence, and I am forever grateful to them."

That was Karin Jean-Pierre, President Biden's press secretary, speaking right after she took the job. Notice the only thing she doesn't talk about are her qualifications for the job. Actual qualifications. Instead, she plays identity politics. As if those are the reasons she got the job.

I have come to hate the word "victim." So overused, so exaggerated, so weaponized to misrepresent reality. I'm not saying there aren't victims. Of course there are. There are real crimes committed against real people every single day. Those are the victims. They are not people who have decided that because they didn't get exactly what they feel entitled to, that they are now victims. Just so we draw the line up front.

I've never understood the idea of wanting something given to you without having properly earned it. Was there a time when white people in this country had more opportunities than black people or other minorities? Yes, there was. Thankfully, much of that has been fixed. And it continues to get better. Were those white people privileged to be born white? No. They were just lucky.

It's not about privilege. It's about executing opportunity in front of you no matter who you are or what your skin color is. Some people just get a head start. That's life. If you lose out to somebody because they outworked you or outperformed you, you have no reason to complain. They just beat you. That's all. When I was playing competitive sports, if someone was better, it didn't matter what skin color they had, they were going to play and I wasn't. I've always loved that sports doesn't adhere to these woke philosophies about privilege and victimhood. If a coach hates your guts, but you are a good player, you will play. Because if the team loses, then the coach may lose his job. Coaches can't afford the luxury of getting all hung up on things like victimhood and privilege.

I wish the rest of the world played at the same stakes, but it doesn't.

I think Karin Jean-Pierre is a good example of what happens when decisions are made not based on talent or ability, but skin color and sexual orientation. Please don't think I'm personally attacking her. I don't know her, I've never met her, and I am merely making observations about what has become increasingly obvious to many people. She is completely in over her head as the Presidential Press Secretary. I believe she got the position because she fit the virtue signals.

Virtue signaling is putting people on a pedestal who don't have the ability to maintain just what they have been put up there for in the first place. Openly gay Black woman. She checks some pretty heavy "woke" boxes. But did anybody ever check to see if she was really good at the job? Can she read a teleprompter? Can she think on her feet? Can she go off script? Can she manage a meeting? So far, the evidence to all of these answers is underwhelming. If I interviewed to be a sports broadcaster for football games and I couldn't cogently put together my thoughts and speak in a clear and concise manner, I wouldn't last through pregame. Would I be the first light-skinned Black guy to be on the show? Maybe. But who cares? If I'm not qualified, I'm not qualified, and I don't deserve the job. I wish people around Jean-Pierre would help her improve, but I'm fairly sure they are not doing that. How do I know? Because she has not improved. In fact, she doubles down when push comes to shove and digs the inexperience hole even deeper. She does not seem open to any kind of criticism or challenges while she is standing up there at the podium. If you criticize her you're automatically being "unfair" and probably racist and sexist and homophobic, along with a bunch of other things I don't have time to list. The problem is, when you get constructive criticism, it makes you better. But you have to be open to that constructive criticism. Neither seems to be happening. Nobody is giving it to her, and if they are, she's outright ignoring it.

When she was hired, we didn't hear much about her qualifications. All we heard about from the media was how Black she was and how lesbian she was. That's what she was being judged on, it appeared. But you can watch five presidential press conferences and they will probably all cover the same issues. Clearly, she's not saying to herself, I have to get better or get out of here. Everyone in her circle has told her how special she is, so why would she listen to critics all of a sudden? When I watch Jean-Pierre, I always see the same uncomfortable passive-aggressive attitude coming from her. She is representing the President of the United States. Then there's the disinformation and gaslighting that goes on, but we'll get to that later.

While we're on the subject, let's also look at Kamala Harris. I think the same rules applied to her. She wasn't chosen because she would make a good vice president. I said she was chosen because then they could say she was the "first Black female vice president." Checked all the boxes. Just like Jean-Pierre has a bad relationship with the press, it seems that Kamala has a bad relationship with the president. Nobody took into account the importance of those relationships and, rather, simply focused on race and gender. Not good. Being grossly underqualified in the real world will hurt you. If a doctor is not good enough, he's not going to be a doctor for very long. The same thing goes for a pilot or construction worker, or a thousand other jobs. But in politics it's different. In politics, it doesn't matter. Politics has become the ultimate virtue signaling playground.

I never wanted to be the first in anything. I never wanted to be the best first Black news contributor on a late-night comedy show. That's not what pushes me. What pushes me on television is what pushed me on the football field, or in the wrestling ring: my motivation to be stronger and better every single day. When I come off the Greg Gutfeld show I want to know how I did. Did the audience enjoy it? Are they responding and reacting? Because if they are not, then I'm in trouble. No one's going to give me a Participation Award at Fox.

What's frustrating is that we have plenty of examples of minorities who earned it the right way. Colin Powell, Barack Obama, Condoleezza Rice—the list goes on. For me, these are people that knew what they were doing and were focused on getting better every day at what they did. Even if I don't agree with them, I respect them because you have to give credit where it is due. Things need to be earned. Why do you think there are riots when they give out free tickets to something? It's because nobody earned it. Nobody had anything invested in it. You just can't give stuff away and not expect there to be consequences.

When I was in the WWE's developmental training program, there was a group of us who were about to get ready for TV. The coaches were looking to us to be the leaders of the next wave of wrestlers because they knew we were approaching the point where we could carry things on our own. We had all worked hard. We had put in the time and the sweat. It was a lot of work, but we all felt like it was about to pay off. Then we got word that somebody was being introduced to our group. He was the son of a well-known wrestler. Like with any situation like this, whether it's football, basketball, or another sport, simply being an offspring doesn't mean you've got the goods to translate into success. In fact, it often doesn't. In wrestling, if you're not a monster or a circus freak show then you have to be in great shape. He wasn't any of these things. He just looked average. Not very athletic, didn't know much about anything. The only reason he was there was because of his dad. We had all sacrificed so much, and now we had to carry this guy on our backs and help get him ready.

It was a tense time all around. We would start doing try-out matches in empty arenas while the tribunal of three or four decision makers sat there judging whether we had what it took to get to the next level. Every day it felt like your ass was on the line and your career could be snuffed out with one bad performance, which was absolutely the case. Then we got a call that a group of agents was coming down to look at us and decide after a series of practice matches who would move on. This kid, this wrestler's son was going to be working with all of the best guys in front of the agents. My partner and I couldn't believe it.

He had done nothing to deserve this. Nothing. So what happened? He didn't do well. Nobody thought he had what it took and so, within a couple of weeks, he bailed. He never had the desire in the first place. He thought he could simply walk in because he was well-connected. He never gave it a second thought that maybe it was going to take some real talent, ability, and effort. But that's the way it goes. He didn't get a participation trophy. That was good. But I never forgot the feeling of watching somebody walk into a situation and be given all kinds of special opportunities simply because of who he was instead of what he was.

That's something that will never sit easy with me.

'Nuff Said

Millennials

I need to talk about millennials in the workplace, and why it seems like pulling teeth to get them to work hard. A lot of my friends in the world that run companies tell me all the time how tough it is when it comes to hiring millennials, when it's already tough enough to run a business.

First off, let's establish who we're talking about here. Millennials, also known as Gen Y, are generally considered to be those born between 1981 and 1996. So if you're reading this and you were born in that timeframe, congratulations, you're a millennial!

Now, let's address the elephant in the room. There's a common perception that millennials are lazy, entitled, and unwilling to work hard. And you know what? There's some truth to that.

Before you start throwing your avocado toast at me, let me explain. It's not that millennials are inherently lazy or entitled. It's that we've grown up in a world where we've been told that we can do anything we want, that we're special and unique snowflakes, and that we deserve the best of everything.

This constant stream of praise and positive reinforcement has had some unintended consequences. It's created a generation of young people who are used to getting what they want, when they want it, without having to work very hard for it.

So when these same millennials enter the workforce, they're often shocked to find that they're not the center of attention anymore. They're not getting constant praise and validation, and they're expected to put in long hours and hard work to succeed.

And that's where the real problem lies. Many millennials simply aren't prepared for the rigors of the working world. They're used to being able to coast by on their natural intelligence and charm, and they're not used to having to put in the hard work to get ahead.

But it's not all the fault of the millennials, either. The working world has changed a lot in the past few decades, and many of the traditional career paths that previous generations followed are no longer viable options.

Gone are the days of working for the same company for thirty years and retiring with a gold watch and a pension. Now, it's all about job-hopping, freelancing, and building a personal brand.

And while these changes have opened up new opportunities for millennials, they've also created a sense of uncertainty and instability. With so much competition and so few guarantees, it's no wonder that many millennials are hesitant to put in the hard work and dedication that traditional career paths require.

So what can be done to get millennials to work hard? Honestly, there's no easy answer. But here are a few suggestions for those that may be hiring:

1. Set clear expectations: If you want millennials to work hard, you need to be crystal clear about what you expect from them. Don't assume that they know what's expected of them—spell it out in black and white.

2. Provide regular feedback: Millennials thrive on feedback—both positive and negative. Regular check-ins and constructive criticism can go a long way in keeping them motivated and engaged.

3. Offer flexibility: Millennials value work-life balance more than any previous generation. Offering flexible schedules, the ability to work from home, and other perks can make them more willing to put in the hard work when they're on the clock.

4. Lead by example: If you want millennials to work hard, you need to lead by example. Be willing to roll up your sleeves and put in the same level of effort and dedication that you're asking of them. If they see that you're willing to work hard, they're more likely to follow suit.

5. Provide opportunities for growth: Millennials are ambitious and eager to learn and grow. Providing opportunities for professional development, training, and advancement can keep them motivated and engaged.

6. Recognize their strengths: Millennials have grown up in a world where everyone gets a trophy, and they're used to being recognized for their achievements. Make sure to recognize their strengths and accomplishments and give them opportunities to shine.

7. Foster a positive company culture: Millennials value a positive and inclusive company culture more than any previous generation. Creating a work environment that's supportive, collaborative, and fun can go a long way in keeping them motivated and engaged.

We can do this. I don't think it's fair for us to just dismiss entire groups of people simply because we don't understand their attitude. They didn't just get that way by accident. It took a village to raise millennials and it's going to take a village to get them straight in the workplace.

Nuff said.

CHAPTER 8

Abortion

We all can agree on this at least: Abortion is a deeply controversial and polarizing issue that has been debated for decades. Some argue that it's a woman's right to choose what happens to her body. Others believe it is morally wrong to end the life of an unborn child. Regardless of where one stands on this issue, it is important to recognize that abortion is a difficult and emotionally charged decision to make. We agree, right?

One obvious reason why abortion is such a horrible choice to have to make is that it can be physically and emotionally painful for the woman undergoing the procedure. Abortion involves the termination of a pregnancy, which can cause physical discomfort, bleeding, and cramping. In some cases, complications may arise that require medical intervention. Additionally, many women who choose to have an abortion experience emotional distress, including feelings of guilt, shame, and sadness.

Another reason why abortion is a difficult decision to make is that it can have long-lasting consequences for the woman and those around her. Women who have abortions may experience long-term physical and psychological effects that can impact their overall health and well-being. Additionally, abortion can strain relationships with partners, family members, and friends, and can create a sense of isolation and loneliness.

Perhaps the most difficult aspect of abortion is the moral and ethical dilemma it presents. Many people believe that life begins at conception, and therefore view abortion as the taking of an innocent life. Others argue that a woman's right to choose what happens to her body should take precedence over the rights of an unborn child. This fundamental disagreement has led to heated debates and deep-seated divisions within society. In the end, the decision to have an abortion is a deeply personal one that should be made with careful consideration and reflection.

More specifically on this topic, I look at things through a prism of the responsibility of men. There's this great line in *The Godfather* that no one ever repeats. Don Corleone, towards the end of his life, talks about men and how he spent his whole life being careful because men have to be careful. Women and children don't have to be careful. What he means by that is there is this unwritten society rule for men, period. You are given the right to vote because as a man you'd be the one picked to go fight the wars. So yes, you got the right to vote first, but you had to pay for it in blood. There was no, "Well, I want to vote, but I don't want the responsibility." No, you're a man. You don't have a choice. You do the right thing or you're not a man. That's how societies kind of worked for men. We don't get to opt out. We don't get the equality of choice. Our rules are simple. Men have consequences no matter what. Even stuff we weren't a part of. We see today, a sense of racism and every other thing that's wrong with society. It's all some white man's fault or what have you. And those men have to burden that. And if they argue it, somehow they're not the same thing. And when I think about abortion, when it comes to men, our choice is simple. If a man goes out on a weekend and parties too hard, and has an affair, let's say, and gets a woman pregnant, everyone will say to him, "Well, you did the time, man up." And you're going to take care of the responsibility. You're going to face the consequences of your actions. Your wife is going to divorce you. You're going to pay child support to her and the woman that you met in a bar for forty-five minutes. You'll be supporting her child.

For the rest of its life.

But I don't want to. It's not fair. Screw that. You're a man. Man up. You have to be accountable. It's attached to you, the very essence of who you are. You don't get a pass. You don't get a "Man, I didn't feel right" or "I didn't like it. Well, I didn't want to do it. She made me do it. I was pressured." Well, that stuff doesn't mean shit when it comes to men. We have to. Everything we do has a consequence. And if we don't take accountability for our actions, we're weak. We're soft. We're not real men. And that's everything. Somebody breaks into your house; you don't look at the woman. The man runs to the front door. He risks his life to save the lives of his wife and children or whomever is in the house, even though he might be just as scared as they are. But if he hid under the bed with the wife and kids, the wife and kids wouldn't be called cowards. They'd be called survivors. He'd be a coward. The rest of his days. No matter what he did, he'll be the guy who hid under the bed with his family and didn't face the guy who broke into the house. That's so. Men don't have the luxury to make choices free of consequences.

When I look at an abortion, the argument of abortion, the celebration of what is a horrible decision. Nobody wants to be in that decision. No one smiles at that. That situation has happened, and now I have to make a decision that's going to affect me for the rest of my life. I know, the extenuating circumstances; someone's raped, incest, molestation, pedophilia. Those are a different category. But when it comes down to a woman's choice, a woman's right, I always kind of look at a man's right and kind of smirk. And when I say that, no one would tell a woman, well, you decide to go out and party this weekend. You did the time. You raise that child or you're not a real woman. They would come down on that man who said that or a woman who said that and told them that they were misogynistic, that they were this, they had all these things wrong with them for telling someone to take accountability for their actions. Now, it seems to the point where a man will go to jail if he doesn't. Man can't abort a child. Can't abort financial responsibility. He has to take responsibility for it whether he wants to or not. There are courts in place to make sure that he does. He doesn't have a choice. Regardless, it's a bad choice. It's not a good thing, somebody making a decision to get an abortion. It's not a celebration. The way that it's put on. Like it's a badge of honor. Like it's all right. My right to get ice cream. My right to get an abortion. I do think a woman should have a choice. But I also think her choices should be the same as ours. Or at least we all can make the same choices together. You can choose to terminate. I should be able to choose to walk away. And vice versa. Now, it sounds kind of cold blooded and harsh, but that's just living in feelings, that's not living in facts and fairness. But this isn't about fairness when it comes to the argument of abortion, where life starts, where life begins. It doesn't really matter if you're choosing to end your pregnancy. It's just you made that decision. You're going to go forward, and you're going to do something really difficult that you're going to have to live with. The rest of your life. Now someone's going to say, who the fuck am I to make a statement like that? There's no winners. When you have to get an abortion, no matter your best intentions or your best reasons for not having the child, there's going to be days where you hear a child laughing and you're going to think, *Did I make the right decision?* The same thing goes for someone who chose to keep a child and raise them, but then they never meet their potential because of the work required to raise a child. Maybe the mom winds up in poverty or is stuck with someone they don't love, then there will be a day where they go, *Man, I wonder what my life would be like if I would have thought differently and not had the kid.*

I pretty much heard my mother say that a million times when she was frustrated. "If only I got an abortion. What would my life be like, what choices could I make?" People say those things in the heat of battle and the heat of life. It doesn't make them a bad person. It just means they're dealing with a shitty situation. Well, how do I know so much about this from a man's perspective? My sophomore year in college, a girl I was dating informed me that she had gotten pregnant. My first reaction was, *Oh, shit*, like anyone else. But my second reaction was, "What do you want to do?" Not, "This is what I want to do." This isn't, hey, we're going to get married, or we're going to have a child, or we'll figure it out, or we'll work together or whatever. Because she didn't come to me with a smile on her face. She came to me cold and pale and sad, eyes swollen from crying. I knew what she had to tell me wasn't going to be something she was excited about. When I asked, what's the biggest issue? And it was a very simple answer. She was concerned about having a Black child in the Midwest. And she didn't know anyone that had a relationship with somebody they went to college with. College is supposed to be about having fun, and then you go home and you marry your hometown sweetheart from high school or whatever. You're not supposed to run off with one of us, so to speak. It's not a racist person, but she lives where she lives and that's her attitude. When I heard this, my thought was, *Why did you even talk to me in the first place if you knew this was a problem?*

As a man, it's like you try to understand. And I said what every most every decent man would say. Because you don't have a choice. You have to be supportive. You can't say, "Hey, what about me? You're not even asking me. You're telling me." I said, "Whatever you want to do, I support you. But maybe we should just sleep on it and talk about it tomorrow." Well, a few days went by, and the only thing she wanted to talk to me about was making an appointment and whether I was going to pay for it. Because the financial responsibility, of course, fell on me, the man, because I'm the one that did the deed. At no time did I hear about her responsibilities. Just her responsibility to get an abortion. It was around $250 or $350. I could come up with it. I knew I had to.

We get chivalrous. We want to protect. We want to be there. And there was even a part of me that thought if I was supportive throughout the process that maybe she would rethink this. I was a full-ride scholarship athlete. I had pro scouts looking at me. I had good grades. I looked at it like it would have been a challenge, but I would be willing to step up. She had little or no faith in me at all in that department. Nothing about me at that particular point when she looked at me in this situation made her feel like "this is the guy." Can't change that. So at the end of the week she had made an appointment. And then it became like a friend was going to drive with us and there were all kinds of emotions. She would have days where she would be crying, and then she would have days where she was like, "Well, what if we keep it?" I could tell that she wasn't sure which way she wanted to go, that she was agonizing, and this was a really difficult decision.

It's a tough decision to be sitting there weighing the pros and cons to keep a life and raise it. Or end it and move on and try to forget about it. That's basically what you're trying to do. And then, as a man, while she's weighing these things, I'm just drifting in the wind. I can't say anything. Anything I say makes me a monster. If I say, "You know what, I don't want this baby either just because of what you said about me." I'm the bastard if I say, "You know what? I'm too young, and I've got my whole career ahead of me. This is a good idea. Here's the money. Let's just get it done." If I say, "I want to keep it," I'm out of my fucking mind. And I have no right to tell a woman that. So my role is purely supportive, whichever direction she decides she wants to go in. That's the best you can do as a man is to be supportive because everything you say is wrong. And then she'll have a friend or someone who says, "You have no idea. It's not your body, it's not your this or that." But it's my time. It's my effort, it's my passion, it's my finances, it's my direction in life. It is being a man and a provider. Those are all the things that are on the table for me. I came from a tough background, but the one thing I didn't ever do in my life was quit. But again, it's not my decision. I keep the money in my pocket.

We drove four hours to the clinic. After walking in, I quietly sat down. If you've ever been in a place where you sat for so long, you hear a high-pitched ping in your ear because you can't hear anything else. Every woman who was sitting in that building was sad. I'm in that waiting room, and I don't belong. But I was going to be there the whole way. I said, "If this is what you want to do, I'll be there to hold your hand. I'll do the right thing." I'm the man till the end, the big protector, even though I felt this was not a good decision. I felt we both knew what we were doing, that either one of us could have gotten a condom. And I felt that we should be doing the right thing, what I thought was the right thing. The right thing for her was to end this and get back to the life she wanted. Running around with me was not it.

I'll never forget sitting there with my head down, the room painted a dull olive green-gray. I was the only man there. I looked across at an older woman who had two of her kids with her. For her, it appeared to be a financial decision. And I'm just sitting there and I'm looking at people trying not to focus on my situation. Then I see a young woman sitting by herself just sniffling and filling out her paperwork, and the girl I was with, she was filling out her paperwork. I'm looking around this room, I'm trying to understand every person in there. There was no one in that waiting room waiting to tell a funny story, nobody with a new article. or great TV series they wanted to share. We all acknowledged each other, but nobody wants to make steady eye contact. This is a horrible, tough decision. Everyone in this waiting room on this day is never going to be the same. You'll move on from it. You'll put it in perspective. But whenever this day comes, you'll remember it.

The office smelled too clean. It was like lemon. It was just sadness in that room.

I put my head down and started thinking maybe she'll realize that this is not where we should be. I saw a woman of poverty. I saw an older woman. I saw a younger woman. Every one of them was alone and sad. Just then they called her name, and she got up and made her way to the back. Her friend tells me I'm not allowed to go with her, so now I'm just sitting there. Everyone was looking at me. I'm the villain. I made her do it. Of course you did, man. Of course, that's what a man does. I put my head down and was just trying to get through it.

Then she comes walking back out. She looks at me, and I get a smile on my face. I'm thinking she's going to tell me she can't go through with it, and let's get out of here. She takes a deep breath and says, "I need the money." I had completely forgotten it was even in my pocket. I was just numb to the whole experience, and, in my softest voice, I said, "Oh, yes. So sorry," reached into my pocket, and handed her the money. I felt like a pimp. I felt gross.

I wasn't judging her. I'm there. I'm supporting her. I don't get to have buyer's remorse. Hindsight is 20/20. I don't get to blame it all on her because that's not what men do. We take it. Everybody hates us, but we're the ones who have to take out the trash. Everybody wants to blame us for everything that's wrong, but we're the ones that feel the heat from the fire. We have to take the dirty looks, get spit on, get our hands dirty to get things clean. We've got to plant the trees we'll never see so someone else can have a good day. That's what a man is in this situation.

She goes back in, and I put my head down. The older woman from across the room came over and sat next to me. "Are you okay?" she asked me. I looked at her and said, "I'm okay. Thank you. Are you okay?" "None of us are okay in here," she said. That has lived with me ever since.

After we exited the clinic, I helped her into the car. She cried the whole way home. She cried for the next two days. I got our assignments from class. I did the good-man thing the whole time. I thought to myself, *There has got to be another way.* But I did not have a voice. My role was simple; be there. I did my man part. That's all our part is in this. It's a woman's right. It's her choice, and she has to live with it. But understand, there was nobody in that room on that day beating on their chest saying, "My right, my right." We need to get back to the civility of understanding that anyone who wakes up in the morning, whether they are devout Christian or an absolute atheist, and is looking in the mirror, thinking about getting an abortion, they are not having a good day.

I'm not judging her now. But I always had this optimism that everything was going to be better, and that probably helped me get to where I am today in life. But she didn't have that with me. After a few weeks had gone by, she came to me and said that she was never going to do that again if we got pregnant, just consider myself a father. That was how she wanted to deal with it. Because she was struggling with the horrible choice: do I end a life or start a life? As a woman, that is the toughest decision on the planet. And I was a witness to it; I saw the damage it did to her and to me. I didn't want to touch her. Not because she was disgusting, not because of anything like that, but because I didn't want to go through that again.

A few years went by. I ran into her in the most random place. She's got two kids, and looks at me, and I see her, and I think. I think we gave each other hugs and I asked her how she was, and she told me that she still hasn't gotten over the decision she made.

I had put it behind me. She had a new life, a new family, and she was still struggling with the decision she had made five years earlier. So it was her right. But she has to live with that. She did what was best, what she thought she had to do. There's a difference. You can have two thoughts on one subject. I feel like I say that all the time, and, in this case, it's never been more true.

Maybe if we all lightened up on and stopped screaming at each other, *Who's gonna be the first in line to kill it or keep it or raise it*, maybe we back up and say, "I'm sorry you had to be in this situation. Whatever happened, how can I help?" Where's the civility? That's essentially what is missing with the whole abortion thing, in my opinion. If you are a man or woman of God, and you are watching somebody who doesn't have your faith make one of the toughest decisions of their life that they're going to have to live with, do you think attacking them helps them? I get it. It's business and people go out and react. I just feel when it comes to abortion, I will never, ever tell a woman what to do with her body. We have no dog in this fight because our rules are set. Any man who lays with a woman and she gets pregnant and keeps it, it's your responsibility because you're a fucking man. You have to be careful and not let things like this happen.

Because if you're not careful, no one's going to let you out of it.

So where does life begin at? Is it the instant the egg meets the sperm? Or is it forty-eight hours later? I don't know. But I *do* think that we need to be asking ourselves, where did our decency go?

CHAPTER 9

Junk Food~the Worst Addiction

Nobody seems to want to talk about it, so I will. America's addiction with junk food.

Why is it such a tough subject to confront?

First, food is a deeply personal and emotional topic. We all have individual relationships with food, which can be influenced by our upbringing, culture, and personal experiences. For many people, food is tied to feelings of comfort and pleasure, even guilt or shame. This can make it challenging to discuss food-related issues in a non-judgmental and open-minded way. I've got my favorite guilty pleasures, don't you?

Next, there is a lot of conflicting information and opinions about food and nutrition. With so many different diets, fads, and studies out there, it can be hard to know what information to trust. This can lead to confusion and frustration when trying to have meaningful conversations about food addiction. And when you look at the relationships the many food companies have with the government, it becomes even harder to separate reality from bullshit.

Also, food addiction is not yet widely recognized as a legitimate condition. While there is growing evidence to support the idea that certain foods can be addictive, it is still not widely accepted by the medical community. (The foods that people are most likely to compulsively overeat have something in common: a potent mix of carbohydrates [such as refined grains and/or sugar] and fat. I'm looking at you, chocolate, pizza, and ice cream!)

Some people don't even believe it exists. When the hell are we going to wake up and address this problem for what it is?

I get that there is a lot of stigma surrounding obesity and overeating. In our culture, there is often a moral judgment attached to being overweight or struggling with food addiction. This can make it difficult for people to talk openly about their experiences and seek help without feeling ashamed or judged. But maybe, just maybe, sometimes we need little moral judgment when it comes to obesity. I'll get to that in a little bit.

I get it. Discussing America's addiction to junk food can be challenging due to the deeply personal and emotional nature of the topic, conflicting information about nutrition, lack of recognition of food addiction as a legitimate condition, and the stigma surrounding obesity and overeating. But we still have to do it.

The United States has been facing an obesity epidemic for many years, and it is a major public health concern that affects people of all ages and socioeconomic backgrounds. One of the most significant contributors to this epidemic is the availability of cheap, processed foods. Fast food restaurants and convenience stores are ubiquitous in American society, and they offer quick and convenient options for meals and snacks. These foods are often high in calories, sugar, and fat, and lack essential nutrients that the body needs to function properly. Additionally, these foods are often marketed to children and young adults, making them appealing to a vulnerable population.

Another factor contributing to America's addiction to food is the culture of overconsumption. Large and oversized portions are commonplace in restaurants, and many people have become accustomed to consuming more food than their bodies need. Additionally, food is often used as a reward or a way to cope with stress or negative emotions, leading to a cycle of emotional eating.

The food industry also plays a significant role, spending billions of dollars each year on advertising and marketing, using tactics such as product placement and celebrity endorsements to promote their products. They also employ food scientists who work to create products that are highly palatable and addictive, making it difficult for people to resist them. As Alexander Heyne wrote at modernhealthmonk.com, *"Hot chocolate, for example, has almost no chocolate in it. It's a high school science experiment. If that terrifies you, it should. It's basically made up of some dairy replacements (for that creamy quality) and then has added sugar and artificial flavors. There are billion dollar businesses designed to make food taste like something that it's not. So instead of including dairy products in your food, the artificial flavoring companies can remove that and just make it taste like there's dairy in there."*

The consequences of America's addiction to food are serious. Obesity is a major risk factor for many chronic diseases, including heart disease, diabetes, and cancer. These diseases not only lead to premature death but also have a significant economic impact on society in the form of health-care costs and lost productivity. In addition to the physical consequences, there are also psychological and social consequences. Many people who struggle with their weight experience low self-esteem and negative body image, leading to depression and anxiety. Socially, people who are overweight or obese often face discrimination and prejudice, which can lead to social isolation and a lack of opportunities.

So when are we supposed to do something about it?

Addressing this addiction requires a multifaceted approach. One of the most effective ways to address it is to promote healthy eating habits and physical activity. This can be done through education and public awareness campaigns that promote the benefits of a healthy diet and regular exercise. Additionally, policies can be put in place to regulate the food industry, such as labeling requirements and restrictions on marketing to children. But I don't think we're going to see that too soon because politics gets in the way.

What can you do to help your own addiction? Definitely seek support from a healthcare provider, join a weight-loss program, or work with a nutritionist to develop a healthy eating plan. Additionally, you can make small changes in your daily life, such as choosing healthier options when eating out or incorporating more physical activity into your routine. One thing I don't think you should do is make excuses for being overweight or worse, feel celebrated. This new trend in modern culture to blow smoke up people's asses and tell them how great they look at 250 pounds, I'm sorry, we are doing them no favors. I'm not saying we publicly shame anybody, but how about a little heart-to-heart behind the scenes? How about confronting reality? Being overweight leads to an early grave. There's no two ways about it.

We talk about the horrors of fentanyl. We talk about the horrors of crack. We talk about the ugliness of alcoholism, the consequences of an addiction to porn or gambling. By far, the worst addiction in this country is to sugar. It's the only addiction everyone's okay with. If you're looking to the government to help you eat healthy, good luck. They're not going to help you. They're going to help whomever is going to pay the highest lobbying fees to get on the dance floor. At this rate, a Snickers bar will be the new meatloaf.

Politics plays a huge role in America's addiction to sugar. Look at the government subsidies for corn: The US government provides subsidies (upwards of $19 billion per year) for corn production, which has led to an abundance of cheap corn syrup. High-fructose corn syrup is a common sweetener used in many processed foods and beverages, and its widespread use has been linked to the rise in obesity and other health problems.

There's the lobbyists for the food industry. The food industry has a significant influence on government policies related to nutrition and public health. Their lobbying efforts shape government regulations and policies, making it easier for companies to market and sell sugary products.

The United States has lax regulations on food marketing, which means that food companies can market sugary products to children and other vulnerable populations in foreign countries. This contributes to excessive consumption of sugary products, which easily leads to health problems. And while the government oversees nutrition education campaigns and recommendations, political pressure influences the content and messaging of these campaigns, which may not always be aligned with the best available science regarding the health risks of consuming too much sugar.

Simply put, the government is not looking out for you when it comes to sugar. Have any times do we hear, "It's not going to hurt you, it's just one slice of cake"? Imagine a guy in rehab for crack. If someone said to him, "Take one hit, man. It's just one hit. It's not going to kill you. Loosen up." What would we say? What about telling an alcoholic who's been sober for three years, "It's just one shot. What are you so scared of?" We need to start putting the most unhealthy processed foods in the same category. I know that sounds counterintuitive because we need food to survive.

Food addiction is not currently recognized as an official diagnosis by the Diagnostic and Statistical Manual of Mental Disorders (DSM-5), but research suggests that it shares many similarities with drug and alcohol addiction in terms of brain reward pathways and behavioral patterns.

Like drug and alcohol addiction, food addiction can lead to cravings, loss of control, and compulsive consumption despite negative consequences. Bottom line? Food addiction should be taken seriously.

There was a time when I ate my issues away. Instead of dealing with life, I would consume more food with lots of sugar. I wish somebody had said to me, "You're unhealthy. You need to fix this now." Thankfully, I did have a friend, an old bodyguard buddy back when I was bouncing clubs, who finally got in my face and got me on the right path to help. Had Instagram been around back then, I'm sure plenty of people would've been saying, "Tyrus, you are so beautiful! Forget what your doctor says. Be proud of your weight. Love you!"

As is the problem with many issues today, we let feelings instead of facts dictate the conversation. So many people today will go to a restaurant, order an appetizer that's a meal in itself, then get an entrée that is twice the size that it needs to be, and dessert. After an hour, they've consumed five thousand calories. Then they go home and binge Netflix for eight hours, get six hours of sleep, get up in the morning, go to Starbucks, and get a thousand-calorie Frappuccino and a cheddar sausage sandwich. Two hours later it's lunch time, so they hit the BK, then snack on a bag of chips before heading home. Repeat seven times a week. You've got people consuming ten thousand calories a day with no exercise, no nothing. And instead of being concerned that they weigh three hundred pounds, they go on social media where everyone tells them they're doing great.

Nobody feels good about being obese. You can lie about it and try to put a positive spin on it but inside, nobody is happy about being a beast. Just like there aren't any happy drunks or cool crackheads. This is where I think it's fair to judge people a little bit. People get so bent out of shape if you bring up the fact that they are overweight. Obesity has become beautiful. If the doctor gets concerned with your weight, he's judging you. If people have a problem with your weight, maybe they are racist. Or misogynist. Look, I've been a biscuit away from five hundred pounds, and I had to work my ass off to get that number down. I always have to watch my weight. That's why I'm always at the gym or riding the bike. I'm doing something to burn calories. And I go to the doctor for regular checkups to make sure my blood pressure and cholesterol are in good shape. Being fat helps nobody. It hurts you, and it hurts the people around you. I know I'm going to get a lot of shit for saying things like this, but I really don't care. We need to address this now. You would think COVID would have helped everyone understand why it's better to weigh less. That was the ultimate wake-up call. People that were overweight were more apt to die during the pandemic. That was a huge contributing factor.

It's an addiction. I get it, it's hard. Your brain is telling you it's okay, eat more sugar and salt. Yet today society rewards food excess. You will see a video of a 400-pound guy on Instagram doing ballet with everybody freaking out and saying how beautiful and wonderful it is. They will never say, imagine how much better it would look if he weighed 120. I know, I know; he has big bones. Don't even get me started on that line of excuses. I have big bones, some of the densest bones you will ever find in a human being, and I'm not using that as an excuse. It's on me.

I saw a video recently of a woman chewing out a Target employee because they didn't carry women's blouses in 5-X sizes. All of a sudden the world needs to adjust to overly obese people, so this lady was blaming Target for not carrying something maybe one in fifty thousand people need. Rather than looking in the mirror and worrying about things like diabetes and heart disease, she went on the attack.

This country is eating itself into an early grave. I'm not saying I want government intervention. Hardly. I'm not saying there should be new rules and laws to prevent you from being fat. I'm just preaching common sense. I'm just talking general health awareness and the risks associated with being fat. Pointing out that somebody is overweight, at least in my opinion, is not fat shaming. It's just like saying to somebody, "Do you really need to smoke three packs of cigarettes a day? Do you know what that's doing your health?" It's just helping someone out.

I used to shame myself when I was overeating. I would pretend I was ordering for more than one person at Burger King. "Yes, I would like a double whopper with cheese meal and then a chicken sandwich meal, two large drinks and a strawberry shake." I would order as if there was somebody next to me. Then I would eat all of it before going to work at the clubs, bouncing. After work was done at the Saddle Ranch, we would get these giant platters, massive amounts of food topped off with peach and apple cobbler. I was eating around the clock and not eating well. The fatter I got, the weaker and more miserable I felt. It went way back for me. As a kid I would sneak eat. It was a coping skill I developed to deal with my dysfunctional family when my mother was with my tormentor, Craig. I coped with all of the pain by eating and hiding food to eat when nobody was looking. My problems with food go way back. And they are steeped in emotional episodes. As I got older, it just spun out of control.

It wasn't until one of my best friends, Rico, confronted me and told me that I was going to be dead by the time I was forty if I didn't stop binging. During my stint as a bodyguard, a close girlfriend dumped me, and that forced me to eat even more. I think I was over 425 pounds. Was I going to hit 500? It was looking pretty likely. So then I started meeting with a buddy at Gold's Gym, and thanks to the pressure he put on me, I was able to work that weight down. But it took somebody being honest and confronting me. That's the thing. I wasn't offended when he came at me. Looking back on it, he kind of saved my life. He cared about me. He knew it wasn't going to be an easy conversation, but that didn't stop him. In the absence of the government or other official organizations stepping into to truly help you balance and maintain a healthy weight, maybe someone around you, someone close to you that you trust will speak up. Or maybe you can do that for somebody else.

Remember, if someone in your life confronts you about your weight or any related health issues, it can be an uncomfortable and difficult conversation to have. However, it's important to keep in mind that this person likely has your best interests at heart and is trying to help you. Be open to these conversations because they can really help.

We may not realize the extent to which our weight or health is impacting our lives. Having someone point out your weight gain can help you become more aware of the problem and motivate you to make changes.

Conversations about weight and health should be approached with kindness and empathy. It's important to listen to the other person's perspective and feelings, and to avoid making judgments or assumptions. But if we care about somebody or if somebody cares about us, it's incumbent upon all of us to confront this serious issue. Again, nobody's really talking about it in the media. Nobody's really talking about it at the government level. This is something I think we need to take control of ourselves, this is an issue that we can change and make it better if we use a little common sense and keep an open mind.

Has all of this talk about food made me crave a giant ice cream sundae? Hell yes. And I going to have one right now? No I'm not. It's all about moderation and self-control. In my opinion, there are many forces today making it all too easy to eat too much of the wrong stuff. As a nation, I think we need to confront this and start developing more responsible dietary options that are both nutritious and affordable for everybody.

𝔑𝔲𝔣𝔣 𝔖𝔞𝔦𝔡

Vegans, Climate Change, and Electric Vehicles

Anyone else tired of obnoxious vegans, climate change alarmists, and electric car enthusiasts who just won't shut up about their causes?

First up, let's talk about vegans. Now, I get it—some people choose to eat a plant-based diet for various reasons, and that's their choice. But what I can't stand is when they start preaching to the rest of us about how meat is murder and how we're destroying the planet by eating it. Look, I love a good steak as much as the next guy, and I'm not going to apologize for that. But these vegans act like they're on some sort of moral high ground, looking down on us mere mortals who dare to enjoy a juicy burger or a crispy piece of bacon. And don't even get me started on the ones who try to push their vegan agenda on their pets. I mean, come on—your dog needs meat, people. It's in their DNA. So, to all you obnoxious vegans out there, I have one message for you: mind your own plate and let the rest of us enjoy our food in peace.

Now, let's move on to the climate change alarmists. Look, I'm not going to deny that climate change is a real issue that we need to address. But what I can't stand is when these alarmists act like it's the only thing that matters, and they're willing to sacrifice everything else to try and fix it. I mean, come on—do you really expect us to believe that the world is going to end in twelve years if we don't immediately stop using fossil fuels and start living like cavemen? And don't even get me started on the ones who try to blame every natural disaster on climate change. Look, hurricanes, wildfires, and floods have been happening for centuries—it's called nature, people. So, to all you climate change alarmists out there, I have one message for you: yes, we need to take action to address climate change, but let's not go overboard and start acting like the world is ending tomorrow.

And finally, let's talk about electric car enthusiasts. Now, I'm not opposed to electric cars—in fact, I think they're a great innovation that has the potential to revolutionize the way we get around. But what I can't stand is when these enthusiasts act like they're the only solution to our transportation problems. I mean, come on—do you really expect us to believe that everyone is going to ditch their gas-guzzlers and switch to electric, no matter what? And don't even get me started on the ones who try to guilt-trip us into buying electric cars by claiming that we're destroying the planet if we don't. Look, electric cars have their own set of issues, like the environmental impact of producing the batteries and the fact that they're not practical for everyone. So, to all you electric car enthusiasts out there, I have one message for you: yes, electric cars are cool, but let's not act like they're the only solution to our transportation problems.

So, what's the bottom line here? It's simple—these obnoxious vegans, climate change alarmists, and electric car enthusiasts need to tone it down a notch. Yes, they're passionate about their causes, and that's great, but they need to learn how to communicate their message without being obnoxious and preachy. Instead of trying to guilt-trip and shame people into their way of thinking, they should try to have respectful conversations that acknowledge different perspectives.

For example, instead of constantly pointing out the negative impacts of meat consumption, vegans could focus on promoting the benefits of a plant-based diet in a positive manner. Similarly, climate change activists could work on finding common ground with those who are skeptical of climate change and focus on advocating for practical solutions that benefit everyone. And electric car enthusiasts could acknowledge that electric cars aren't a perfect solution for everyone and work on promoting a variety of environmentally friendly transportation options.

People, everyone has the right to their own beliefs and causes, but it's important to remember that preaching too hard about them can be obnoxious and turn people off. So let's all try to communicate our messages in a respectful and positive manner, and work together to find solutions that benefit everyone. And if you can't do that, then you may need to take a step back and reevaluate your approach, because no one likes an obnoxious know-it-all.

Nuff said.

CHAPTER 10

In Defense of Cops

There's a lot of talk these days about police brutality, corruption, and all sorts of other negative stuff. And yeah, I get it, some cops have made some pretty big mistakes in the past. But here's the thing: we need to support the police, even when they screw up. And I'm gonna tell you why.

First of all, let's get one thing straight: being a police officer is not an easy job. These guys and gals put their lives on the line every single day to keep us safe. They deal with some of the worst people in society, and they often do it with a smile on their face. They work long hours, they miss holidays with their families, and they do it all for us. So the least we can do is show them a little respect.

Now, I'm not saying that we should blindly support the police no matter what. If a cop does something wrong, they should be held accountable for their actions. But here's the thing: mistakes happen. We're all human, and we all make mistakes. Cops are no different. And when they do make mistakes, we can't decide that all cops are bad.

Think about it: if you were in a life-or-death situation, who would you want there to help you? The police, that's who. They're the ones who are trained to deal with all sorts of emergencies, from car accidents to violent crimes. They're the ones who know how to keep us safe. And yeah, sometimes they're gonna make mistakes. But would you rather they didn't do anything at all? I didn't think so.

Plus, let's not forget that the police are an important part of our justice system. They're the ones who catch the bad guys and bring them to justice. Without them, our society would be in chaos. So when we support the police, we're really supporting the rule of law. We're saying that we believe in justice, and that we're willing to do whatever it takes to uphold it.

And finally, let's talk about the bigger picture. When we support the police, we're sending a message to our communities that we care about safety and security. We're saying that we want to live in a world where people can walk down the street without fear of being mugged or assaulted. We're saying that we believe in a better future for ourselves and our children.

So yeah, some cops have made some mistakes in the past. Who hasn't? We're all human, after all. And when it comes down to it, the police are the ones who keep us safe. They're the ones who are willing to put their lives on the line for us every single day. So the least we can do is show them a little respect and support. Because without them, we'd be lost.

I will tell two stories. I will tell the story of when I was on the wrong side of it. And I will tell one when I was on the right side of it.

When I was around twenty-two, I flew home for the summer for a week to see my friends from school. My friend Andre, who was a little older, went to USC and played some ball with the Raiders. and he was friends with Big Corn and those guys. And I went down to see the homies and everything, and he was all, "Yo, just hang with me in my house." He was the only one who didn't work during the day because he worked at clubs at night. So I hung out with him for the day. We went out to get something to eat, and, as we were driving home, we noticed we were being followed by a police car. I said, "Are you speeding?" He's like, "Nope." We got off the exit, pulled into his condominium, got out, and the police car just drove by slowly. We walked into the house and didn't think anything more of it. We were going to play *Madden* on PlayStation.

About an hour later, his front door is kicked in and it's at least ten cops swarming inside.

Some were highway patrol officers. I thought that was weird. A couple had jackets on that said Police. Before I could move, before I could even look up, I heard "Freeze! Don't you move or I'll blow your fucking head off." I had the shiniest gun I had ever seen within three feet of me pulled and ready to go. All I had to do was move and my life was over. There was no question in my mind. With my joystick in my hand, I put my hands up. My head was down. And he's saying, "Get on the goddamn ground."

I go to get on the ground, and the other two cops jumped on me. One stepped on the back of my neck. I was not resisting at all. They tried to put handcuffs on me, but my wrists were too big, so they put zip ties around them that damn near cut my circulation off. Then they dragged me through the front door. They wouldn't even let me stand up, telling me if I moved they would shoot me.

I pushed myself up on my feet as the two cops had me by each arm and walked me out the front door. The cop who'd put his foot on my neck trips me, and I go headfirst onto the concrete. I can't put my arms to block my fall, so I just eat shit on the concrete. He then kneels down and puts his gun right to my temple. I can feel the steel. I can feel the hole right on my eyebrow.

"Where are your drugs?" he said.

I said, "Officer, I don't have any drugs. I'm home from school visiting my friend."

"Where are the stolen cars?"

As I went to answer him, he tapped my temple with that gun. And I'm being affectionately nice when I say tapped.

He said, "You better answer right. Because we're asking him the same questions and whose ever answers are wrong, that one's going to jail. So, where are the stolen cars?"

"I have no idea, officer. I was inside a house playing a video game when you guys came in. I was in Kearney, Nebraska, this time yesterday. I just got home. I don't own a car."

He then used his gun on my temple to help himself stand up. He put the full weight of his body into that gun and pushed off my face before walking back to the house.

My rights were not being read to me. I was not being told why I was being arrested, or why I was being treated the way I was being treated. I lay face down on that concrete for what seemed like forever. I had ants crawling on me, going up my nose and in my ears. There was dust on my face, but I was not going to move because I knew if I moved, it might be the last thing I ever did.

He comes walking back out and kneels down to me again, pulls his gun out again, and says, "So you have no idea where the drugs are?"

I said, "I have no idea, officer. Is that why I'm being arrested? Am I being arrested for drug possession? Because I don't have any drugs on me. I don't do drugs. I haven't drunk anything."

Before I can even finish my sentence, he stands up and says, "I can't hear him that well."

I had a mouthful of dirt, basically, because I was breathing in and breathing out with my face on the ground, so he decided to turn me over on my side. Then he kicked me and told me to turn over. I don't know if you've ever tried to turn over with your hands behind your back. It is not an easy task to do. Then he kicked me in the side of my ribs. Turned me over. "I'm not fucking around with you. You're already going to jail. It's just how you're going to jail that needs to be determined."

"What law did I break?" I asked quietly.

He kicked me again. At that point, I stopped talking. There was no point in me saying anything anymore.

He went back into the house. After a couple of minutes, another cop came out and said, "Hey, hey, kid. What's it say on your shirt?"

I said, "University of Nebraska at Kearney, officer."

He said, "Oh, shit. Maybe he is telling the truth."

Then Dre came out handcuffed. His nose was bleeding, and he said, "Hey, man. He's a kid. He's got nothing to do with this."

The cop said, "Well, where are the stolen cars?"

Dre said, "You're ripping apart my house. You're going through my safe. You're going through all my things. You're taking money out of my bedroom. I don't think there are any stolen cars."

I didn't see Dre get beat up, but he's a big dude, six foot four. I'm still in zip ties lying on the ground. I remember the concrete being hot, like being on the pavement in the summer, like you're at the beach. By this time, I had a puddle on my shirt, and they kept asking me about drugs, and would I take a test. Have I been in jail before? The answer. I have not been to jail, and no, I didn't have any drugs on me. I didn't have any drugs in my system. I said, yeah, I'd take a test, whatever they wanted. I just wanted to go home.

So, I'm agreeing to everything they're asking of me, and it was like there was almost a comfortable warmness to the ground because it was now quiet, and I thought that maybe it was over. I was lying there waiting, blowing ants away from my face.

After a while, the two cops came back. The one that had kicked me a couple of times and put the gun to my head grabbed me and sat me up.

"Your buddy's going to jail," he said. "For resisting arrest, failure to comply, and expired tags on a car. We're searching his house."

They didn't find what they were looking for. Apparently, he didn't have it. Then they took the zip ties off me. My hands were asleep, and I had deep marks in my wrists. I stood up, and the cop had the nerve to ask me, "What's your major, kid?"

Joking, I said, "Law enforcement."

He kind of smirked and said, "Well, you got a crash course in it. You know, you need to pick your friends more careful now."

I didn't want to make eye contact because all I really wanted to do was put my hands on this guy. You know, it would have been a straight up one-on-one. I would have smoked him, but there's a "just get it over with" mentality that kicks in. I had a pretty good idea that I wasn't going to be carted off to jail. Then they said, "Do you have a ride home?"

I said, "No. Am I free to go?"

They said, "Yeah, you're free to go."

I started walking. I had no idea where I was going, I just needed to get as far away from them as possible. I sat on the corner of the street with bug stings on my face, dirt in my hair, and a mark on my temple. With one exception, that was probably the closest I've ever felt to death. Putting a gun to somebody's head and banging them around with it, your finger slips and I'm done, you know? That bothered me for a while. Every time I saw a police car in LA, I'd be fixated on it, worried about driving, making sure I had my license, my insurance, every possible excuse not to get fucked with. That was a difficult time. My biggest beef with the other sheriffs was, when that guy kicked me, someone could have said something because my arms were already tied. I was completely compliant. I was frustrated that no one said, "Hey, man, leave the kid alone." But it didn't happen. To this day, I think of that cop who roughed me up as someone who does not deserve to wear a badge. He doesn't represent the entire force, obviously, but that was a bad guy.

But there's another thing that happened to me around that time that helped offset the feelings I was having when I was working as a bodyguard at a club in Los Angeles.

I'm driving home and it's maybe three o'clock in the morning. The Explorer I'm driving is a total piece of shit and breaks down on the side of the freeway. I'm just a few miles from my house. Bad scenario. I'm on the 101, but as the car started to die I made sure I got over to the shoulder right near the next exit. I'm not sure what to do because money is very tight at this point. I figure I've got to walk down the exit, find a phone to call a tow truck or something. I'm pissed off, but whatever. Just another night, I will figure it out.

I start walking, but I don't think I'm a hundred feet away from the car when I hear the sirens kick in. I'm like, *Fuck me.* The cop pulls over, and the first thing I do is put my hands in the air because I know the routine. It hasn't even been a year since I was thrown down to the ground with a gun to my head at Dre's place, so I'm just thinking, *Here we go again.* I hear the cop on his loudspeaker ordering me to stop walking, so, of course, I do. I just assume I'm going to get fucked with. As he gets out of his car, with my hands up in the air, I take a knee, because I know my height is going to be a problem. I've had these issues before. I *look* like trouble.

I take a knee, and the police officer says, "Sir, is everything okay?"

I say, "I don't know, is it, officer?"

The cop says, "Have you been arrested before or something?"

I say, "No, I'm just big. And whenever I get pulled over, they always want me to put my hands up. So I'm just trying to not be a threat. I don't want any trouble. My car broke down. I'm having a really bad night. I'm just trying to walk to get to a gas station."

He says, "Son, please stand up." I stand up and he says, "Listen, do you know why I pulled you over? It's not safe to be walking on this freeway at night. These trucks are not going to see you. There's a good chance that you can get hit." Then he asks, "What's the problem with your car?"

I'm taken aback. I'm feeling like this is some kind of joke; he wants to search my car. I say, "You're welcome to search my car. I don't have any drugs or anything like that."

He says, "Well, that's good to know. I'm just trying to say, what's the problem with your car?"

I say, "I honestly don't know. It could be out of gas because my gas meter is broken. It could be my battery. I just don't know."

"I'll tell you what I'll do," he says. "I'm going to call a tow truck. I'll give you a ride home myself."

I'm thinking this has to be a trap. I barely fit in the back seat of the car. At this point, if I say no, I don't want a ride, then I feel like I'm vulnerable again. The whole time I'm on edge waiting for the bad apple to appear. Then I ask him, "How much is the tow truck? I don't think I can afford it. I have like sixty bucks cash on me and not a penny to my name. No checkbook, no checking account. I cash my checks when I get them at a check-cashing place. I'm not living the best life right now financially, like I'm week to week bouncing clubs, trying to find a way."

He says, "I didn't say anything about charging, son."

We sit out there for a while. The tow truck comes and hooks up my car, then the police officer drives me to my house. The tow is $260. I say to the cop, "How am I going to pay this?"

He says, "Son. I'm going to take care of this. Obviously, you've had some bad experiences with police officers. Your record is clean. We're not like that. I'm helping you out. I have a son your age." Then he gives me his card. "If you need any help or whatever, just give me a call."

I'm like, *Wow*. I was still waiting for the part where he's gonna club me in the stomach. I say, "Thank you very much, officer."

He says, "No problem, man. That's part of our job. We're not all bad."

And he was white. White as snow. Couldn't have been any whiter. I was thinking, *Wow, he really went above and beyond to help me out.* He didn't have to help me at all. He could have just kept driving, or he could have given me a ticket for leaving the car on the side of the road because in California, you can get a ticket for abandoning your vehicle. I was just taken aback by that. Within a year, I'd gone from one extreme to another.

I can't stress enough that my interactions with police officers over the years have been predominantly positive. Then again, I know to comply when I am approached or confronted by the law. I don't fight back. They are the ones in charge, not me. I think a lot of people today can learn from that approach. Basic common sense. Don't mouth off, don't resist arrest, and don't run away. Look, something bad may still happen. Sadly, there will always be bad officers just like every profession has bad actors. But you can't judge the group based on the bad seeds.

Defunding the police is one of the worst ideas in American history. It's completely one-sided. You will never hear anybody on the right make a case for defunding the police or anything even close to it. I don't think many people on the left were that crazy about it either. The party was hijacked by a bunch of progressive extremists that could give a rat's ass about average, everyday Americans just trying to get by. They seized upon an opportunity and tried to exploit the life of a Black man who was unjustly killed. In my view, that's racist.

Completely unacceptable. But they will never see it that way. They are so selfish and so calculating that all they will ever see is their own political agenda and underhanded motives. Next time you see a cop, do what I do. Ask how they are doing. Tell them to be safe out there. And, if possible, buy them lunch. Just show them that you are grateful for what they do out there every day.

If you are reading this book right now, and you are a member of the law enforcement community, here's an open letter to you, from me:

I am writing this message to express my heartfelt gratitude for the incredible work that you do every single day. Your dedication and commitment to keeping our communities safe and secure is truly commendable and greatly appreciated.

As a member of society, I can only imagine the challenges and risks that come with the job of being a law enforcement officer. You put your lives on the line every day to ensure that we can live our lives with peace of mind and without fear of harm. It takes a special kind of courage and selflessness to do what you do, and for that, I am truly grateful.

Your unwavering commitment to serve and protect is a testament to your professionalism and sense of duty. You work tirelessly in all kinds of weather and at all hours of the day and night, responding to emergencies, investigating crimes, and maintaining order in our communities. Your work not only ensures the safety of our citizens, but also contributes to the overall well-being of society.

I understand that your job is not an easy one, and that you face many challenges on a daily basis. But despite the difficulties, you remain steadfast in your mission to serve and protect. Your dedication and bravery do not go unnoticed, and I want to express my sincere appreciation for everything that you do.

Please know that your hard work and sacrifice does not go unnoticed. You are the unsung heroes who keep our communities safe and secure, and for that, I thank you from the bottom of my heart. Keep up the great work, and may you stay safe and healthy in all that you do.

Sincerely,
Tyrus

𝕹𝖚𝖋𝖋 𝕾𝖆𝖎𝖉

Early Release of Criminals

Let's talk about why criminals end up in jail in the first place. Newsflash: it's because they broke the law! They made a choice to engage in criminal activity, and now they have to face the consequences. So, why on earth would we consider letting them out early?

Some people out there seem to think that we need to be more compassionate towards criminals. They argue that we should focus on rehabilitation instead of punishment, and that allowing early release is a way to encourage good behavior and give offenders a second chance.

Well, let me tell you something, folks: that's a load of BS. Sure, rehabilitation is important, but it doesn't mean we should go easy on criminals. They need to understand that their actions have consequences, and that they can't just get away with breaking the law. Allowing early release sends the message that we're not serious about enforcing the law, and that we're willing to compromise the safety of our communities just to save a few bucks on prison costs.

Let's not forget that criminals are a danger to society. They've already proven that they're willing to break the law, and there's no guarantee that they won't do it again. In fact, many repeat offenders are released early from jail only to commit more crimes and end up back behind bars. By letting them out early, we're putting innocent people at risk.

And what about the victims of crime? Do they not deserve justice? Allowing criminals to leave jail early is a slap in the face to those who have been wronged. It sends the message that their suffering doesn't matter, and that the criminal's "rehabilitation" is more important than their right to feel safe and secure.

Now, some bleeding-heart liberals might argue that we need to focus on rehabilitation in order to reduce recidivism rates. They might say that by providing inmates with education, job training, and counseling, we can help them turn their lives around and become productive members of society.

You know what? They're not entirely wrong. Rehabilitation programs can be effective in helping offenders make positive changes in their lives. But here's the thing: we can't sacrifice the safety of our communities in the process. Think about it: if we release a criminal early and they go on to commit more crimes, what good did our rehabilitation program do? We've put innocent people at risk, and that's simply unacceptable.

And let's not forget about the practical concerns. Yes, prison overcrowding is a real problem, but it's not one that should be solved by letting criminals out early. Instead, we need to invest in more prison facilities and hire more staff to ensure that inmates are properly supervised and that our communities remain safe.

Some might argue that early release programs are necessary to save money. After all, it costs a lot to keep someone in jail, right? Well, yes, it does. But the cost of crime is even higher. When criminals are released early and go on to commit more crimes, we have to spend even more money on law enforcement, court proceedings, and victim assistance. It's a lose-lose situation.

Let's talk about fairness for a moment. If we start letting some criminals out early, where do we draw the line? Who gets to decide which offenders are deserving of early release and who are not? It opens up a whole can of worms and raises serious questions about the integrity of our justice system.

Then there's the message we're sending to our law-abiding citizens. If we start letting criminals out early, what does that say about the value we place on following the law? It undermines the very foundation of our society and erodes the public's trust in our justice system.

Now, some might argue that there are certain circumstances where early release is justified, such as in cases of terminal illness or extreme old age. And while those situations are certainly tragic, they are the exceptions, not the rule. We can't let exceptions dictate our overall policy.

No, folks, the bottom line is this: criminals should serve out their entire sentences. They made the choice to break the law, and they have to face the consequences. If we want to be serious about reducing crime and protecting our communities, we need to be tough on criminals and send a clear message that their behavior won't be tolerated.

Of course, this doesn't mean that we should neglect rehabilitation programs. In fact, we should be investing more in these programs to help offenders turn their lives around and become productive members of society. But we can't sacrifice the safety of our communities in the process.

I'm all for prison reform. Prison reform is if you are in jail for a ridiculous amount of years based simply on drug use/addiction. Then, I think there's a better place for you. Giving somebody twenty years for marijuana possession or selling weed is absolutely nuts. But a man who rapes, is arrested for grand theft, commits manslaughter or murder... No, you serve your time.

I get the good behavior thing. That's what parole boards are for. But if you're arguing for early release because you want to clear up space or you just want to forgive a person for making bad choices in his life because his daddy didn't love him or the system's against them? Bullshit. It's called accountability. Life's not fair. It's not supposed to be fair. No one ever said it was going to be fair. You're still responsible, and you've still got to make good choices. The criminal who willfully beats a small Asian woman to death for her purse? That dude has no business being in society, period.

And yes, George Soros is helping to place in office DAs who believe in early release for bad people. He is a socialist, and he likes playing chess with human beings. If you attack Soros, you're accused of being anti-Semitic? But here's the good news. The American people are fighting back. They are wise to this. They are recalling some of the worst of these Soros DAs. In so many of these great cities today, you can't walk down the street without stepping in shit or tripping on a needle or three or being attacked or robbed by someone who's going to be out of jail by the end of the afternoon because they're not going to process them. If you make bad choices, whether you're white, black, orange, or the color of a baboon's ass, if you make bad choices, if you harm another American citizen, murder them, rob them, rape them, beat them, you need to serve a fair sentence for those behaviors. And if you're a repeat offender, if you've been arrested for assault five, six, seven times; you're done. You need to spend your life incarcerated because you're not safe. It's not fair to American citizens.

It goes back to who are usually the targets. It's not me. I'm not getting snatched up in the street or thrown in the subway, getting a beating in the corner, or robbed or raped. It's women primarily who are being targeted, along with our elderly and store owners.

Simple premise. If you do the crime, you do the time. Especially when it comes to violent, unprovoked attacks on unsuspecting, innocent people.

Nuff said.

CHAPTER 11

Bullying

This one really matters. Look, I may not get bullied today, but it still bothers me. Let me break it down in general terms first: Bullying is a widespread issue that has affected millions of people around the world. It is defined as "repeated aggressive behavior towards someone who is perceived to be weaker or vulnerable." We've all seen it. Bullying can take many forms, including physical, verbal, or emotional abuse, and it can occur in various settings, such as schools, workplaces, or online platforms, no matter what age, sex, or ethnicity.

Bullying is a terrible problem because it has severe consequences for the victim, the bully, and the community as a whole.

First, bullying can have a profound impact on the mental health of the victim. Bullying victims often experience feelings of fear, anxiety, depression, and helplessness. They may also develop low self-esteem and a negative self-image. The trauma of being bullied can stay with a person for a long time, leading to lifelong mental health issues such as post-traumatic stress disorder (PTSD) and anxiety disorders.

Also, bullying can also have significant effects on the victim's physical health. Victims of bullying may suffer from physical injuries such as bruises, cuts, and fractures. The stress of being bullied can lead to various health problems, such as headaches, stomach pains, and sleep disorders. Some studies have even found that victims of bullying have a higher risk of developing chronic illnesses such as heart disease and diabetes later in life.

Bullying can also have a detrimental effect on the social relationships of the victim. Bullying can isolate the victim and make them feel excluded from social groups. This can lead to a lack of trust in others and difficulty in forming new relationships. The victim may also feel embarrassed or ashamed to discuss their experiences, leading to further isolation and social withdrawal. In some cases, victims may even resort to self-harm or suicide due to the overwhelming feelings of loneliness and despair.

Bullying can also have negative consequences on academic performance when students are involved. Bullying can cause a victim to become distracted from their studies and fall behind in their coursework. Victims may also experience a decline in motivation and a loss of interest in school, leading to poor grades and a lower likelihood of graduating. The long-term effects of bullying on academic performance can be devastating, limiting the victim's future career and educational opportunities.

And yeah, bullying can also have a significant impact on the bully. Bullying behavior is often a sign of underlying emotional or psychological issues that require professional intervention. Pity the fools! Bullying can also cause the bully to develop negative behaviors and attitudes towards others, leading to a higher risk of criminal behavior and substance abuse. Additionally, bullying behavior can affect the bully's social relationships and academic performance, leading to a lifetime of negative consequences.

We all know bullying also has a negative impact on the community as a whole. Communities with high rates of bullying often have lower levels of social cohesion and trust. Additionally, bullying can lead to a decrease in school attendance, an increase in crime rates, and a decrease in the quality of life for the community's residents. Communities must take a proactive approach to address bullying and create a safe and supportive environment for all members. It. Is. *Bad.*

It is essential to raise awareness about the negative impact of bullying and take proactive steps to prevent it from happening. Common sense. Moving away from the "academic" take on bullying, how has bullying changed over the years since I was a kid?

Well, bullying is different today because it lasts longer. Maybe not as much for boys; it's oftentimes physical, so you fight at school, the park or wherever, then you go home and it's over. But for a lot of people now, the bullying takes place on social media, which means it runs 24/7. You don't get a break; somebody makes fun of you if you get a spaghetti stain on your shirt. Someone takes a picture of it at lunch, sends it all over school and you get made fun of. And then as soon as you get home, someone's made it their avatar. It doesn't turn off like it did before. When I was growing up, you got bullied, you got off the bus, you got home, you got a break. You could put it behind you and deal with it. You didn't have to deal with the bully cyberbullying you. It's different today. You've got to put them on blast. You've got to tell everybody because after a while, they're going to get tired of messing with you. The problem is that we have the criminals and cowards making the rules in this country. We have a generation of people who think Scarface was a good guy. He was cool.

You always hear the catchphrase "snitches get stitches." That's criminal. That's prison talk. But it's fashionable. It sounds good. And when you feed your kids that type of bull-shit and then wonder why they don't say anything when someone's bullying them or touching them or messing with them it's because we put the wrong value on the wrong things. When's the last time somebody praised the kid for turning in a bully? When was the last time a school had an award for somebody who was in the hall and stopped somebody from being bullied? You never see it. You never see the transition in Hollywood that they'll change the bully. They'll make the bully dumb on TV. But bullies aren't dumb. They're conniv-ing. And, often, they're victims themselves. But we made it so easy to be a bully now because if somebody tells, they get rid-iculed for telling, where instead, we should be praising them. We don't live in that 1950s era anymore. We're not mobsters. No matter how much you want to be on your Instagram, when you crouch down in front of your rented car or whatever the fuck your deal is, trying to look gangster or cool—all that fake shit that you do—and when you're a parent and you're push-ing those values on your kids, you wonder why.

We need to start praising law and order again, we need to start praising virtues, and while I'm not a religious guy at all, I have no problem telling my child to stand up and act straight or virtuous. If pushing the message of religion or whatever it is that makes them good, upstanding young adults, I would support that. And then I'll have the conversation with them on religion if they want to. But the point is, we've pushed the wrong shit. You want to stop a bully? As soon as a bully messes with you, go straight to the teacher. The bully is in the principal's office. The bully is blasted everywhere. That's what needs to happen. But it doesn't. Does he get suspended today? Nope. We don't do that anymore in elementary schools. The attitude is, "Don't say anything." That's what we see on TV. "Don't say anything. I don't want this to happen." And I'll hear someone say, "Oh, he said, if I talk, he's going to beat my mom up." When I was growing up, if you said something about my mama, that was your ass. Like, we're going to fight, and we'll fight again. And here's the deal. I might even lose the fight. I didn't care. I'd fight him again. After a while, it wasn't worth it.

With my kids, I'm like, "Tell on everything." I preach it. I reward it. Someone said something sideways to my son at a baseball game. My son told. He walked over to me and said, "That guy was calling me names," and I was like, "All right. Cool." I went over to the coach and said, "What are we doing here?" That kid got benched for the rest of the game. I didn't get stitches. My son came to me with a problem. I handled it like an adult. I didn't go whoop the coach's ass. I said "Hey, you've got a kid over here cussing and calling people names. What are you going to do about it, Coach?"

I took the bully out of the game. Now, he can't whisper cuss words anymore because he has to sit next to his mom and miss the game. Do you think he's going to say something to another kid again? No. If he threatens my son, he'll just tell me again.

That's the thing with bullying. It's not that bullying is worse. It's just we're lazy in how we deal with it. If a man dressed like a clown stood outside your house and said he wanted to talk to your son or daughter about safe sex, you would lay that dude out in the yard. You would call the police. You would not allow him access to your house. But now that clown doesn't have to knock on your door. He just has to show up in a video game chat, or in your child's social media feed.

It might take him a couple extra days. But he's not only going to get in there, he's going to groom. He's going to create secrets. He's going to convince this child they're talking to another child. But we're still living on that plane where bad guys come through the front door. They're on the platforms. The bullies are there, and we're not looking for them because of our own shit. Every bully I ever had ended one of two ways. I punched him. Or I outgrew him.

When I first moved to California, on the street we lived, there were a bunch of older kids who had bikes, and they would ride their bikes when the kids would be walking home from school, and they'd ride up alongside of them and punch them. I mean, it was like they called it an initiation to their group or whatever.

One day, I was walking with a couple other kids in the rain, and they came up behind one of the other kids and kicked him and knocked him into a puddle of water. I remember he hit the ground pretty hard. As one of the other kids rode by, I kicked his bike. He fell over and he got twisted, his foot caught in the chain. I took off running and the rest of the kids on the bikes tried to chase me. I got home to my backyard, and they were like, "You wanna come out?" For three days they just kept it up. It was all weekend. They kept riding by looking for me. I didn't want to go outside. Every time I went outside, these older kids were threatening to beat me up.

Then one of them came to my doorstep. I was standing just inside the door. I saw my brother was afraid, and I'm like, we're not going to be afraid of this one kid, man. Fuck this. I opened the door as soon as he went to say something and punched him. I just assumed he was there for drama. I was not going to be bullied anymore. I was not going to be bullied in my own house. He was trying to crawl and get away. As I was standing over him and hitting him, one of the other kids came, and I think my brother grabbed a bat or something. I think he was going to hit him in the knee or something like that. And the other kids were like, "You do that, you're going to go to jail." All of a sudden they were all lawyers.

I was like, "Get the hell off my driveway." They left and didn't bother us anymore. After a while, meaning by the weekend, because kids were different back then, they were like, "Hey, do you want to play tag football?" We ended up becoming friends because that's what boys do when they fight. But I was never really afraid of bullies because, after my biological father and what was coming eventually coming with Craig, a regular-kid bully was nothing I was worried about. Unfortunately, because of the violence I was exposed to as a child with my biological father, the average bully was going to have a bad day with me. I didn't want to start trouble, but I had no problem being in trouble.

I remember the kid that I had punched in the face, I split his lip and we wound up best friends. And he would boast, "Oh, this, this dude hit me right here. He's younger than me. He split my lip." I never understood that, but we were friends for a long time.

Every bully I ever ran into, things always ended up the same. We would get into a fight, and we would become friends.

So I just didn't really have a lot of bullying, and I never was a bully myself. I never wanted to bully anybody. And I had real problems. I didn't want to make myself feel better at somebody else's expense, which is basically what a bully does.

We see a lot of that now. We see it on TV. Bullies and cowards surround us. In media entertainment, a man loses his job and somebody on the rival network jumps up in the air to scream and cheer. Cowards love to see heroes fall. Bad people love to see good people fall. Somebody that kicked your ass in the ratings, and you're dancing and singing, and they have a family. You know, those are unfortunately bullies and cowards, and they're going to be everywhere because it's the easiest thing to do, especially with social media, because you can do it anonymously.

Message is: Tell, man! Be a tattletale. Be that punk. Every time somebody comes at me, I'd be like, here's his address. License plate on his car when he came by! Tell! I tell my kids all the time. You sing. You tell me as soon as somebody messes with you. You're in trouble if you *don't* tell me.

𝔑𝔲𝔣𝔣 𝔖𝔞𝔦𝔡

In Defense of Wrestling

I'm a wrestler. I grew up a wrestling fan. So that's why we're about to talk about why pro wrestling will always be an important part of our culture. It's not just because of the flashy costumes, the larger-than-life personalities, or the epic battles in the ring. Pro wrestling is so much more than that. It's a unique form of entertainment that has evolved over the years to become one of the most popular and enduring forms of sports entertainment in the world.

Wrestling was started in carnivals because guys used to bare-knuckle fist fight all over the country, and they'd knock each other's teeth out and give each other black eyes or damn near kill each other. They got together and said, "Listen, I'll let you win next week. I win this week, and we can keep fighting and keep making money and people get to see us every week."

First and foremost, pro wrestling is a form of storytelling. At its core, it's all about good versus evil, heroes versus villains, and overcoming obstacles to achieve victory. These are themes that have resonated with people for centuries, and they continue to captivate audiences in the world of pro wrestling. Whether it's the classic rivalry between Hulk Hogan and Andre the Giant, or the more recent feud between John Cena and The Rock, pro wrestling is filled with iconic stories that have become part of our cultural lexicon.

It's not just the stories that make pro wrestling so compelling. It's the way they're told. Pro wrestling is a unique blend of athleticism, theater, and improvisation. The performers in the ring are not just athletes, they're actors, stunt performers, and storytellers all rolled into one. They use their bodies to convey emotion, they improvise on the fly to create exciting moments, and they work together to tell a cohesive story that keeps audiences on the edge of their seats.

And let's not forget the spectacle. Pro wrestling is known for its over-the-top entrances, elaborate costumes, and pyrotechnics. It's a visual feast that appeals to our sense of spectacle and wonder. There's something truly magical about seeing a wrestler emerge from the smoke and flames, accompanied by their signature theme music, ready to do battle in the ring.

But pro wrestling isn't just about the showmanship. It's also a reflection of our society and our culture. Pro wrestling has always been a mirror that reflects the values, fears, and aspirations of the audience. From the patriotic heroics of Hulk Hogan in the '80s to the anti-authoritarian rebellion of Stone Cold Steve Austin in the '90s, pro wrestling has always tapped into the cultural zeitgeist of the time.

And while the stories and characters may be fictional, the emotions they evoke are very real. Pro wrestling has always been a form of catharsis for audiences. It allows us to experience the thrill of victory and the agony of defeat vicariously through the wrestlers in the ring. It's a way to release our pent-up emotions in a safe and controlled environment, and it's a way to connect with others who share our passion for this unique form of entertainment.

Perhaps the most important reason why pro wrestling will always be an important part of our culture is because of its ability to bring people together. Pro wrestling has always been a communal experience, whether it's gathering around the TV with friends and family to watch WrestleMania or attending a live event with thousands of other fans. It's a shared experience that creates a sense of belonging and camaraderie.

In a world that seems increasingly divided, that sense of community is more important than ever. Pro wrestling provides a space where people from all walks of life can come together and share a common love for this unique form of entertainment. It's a reminder that no matter our differences, we can all come together and enjoy something that brings us joy and excitement.

I knew as a kid: wrestling became popular because you got to see heroes and bigger-than-life characters. And they were there every week. Boxing? You only got to see your favorite fighter maybe once every three months. The NFL, sixteen weeks. Baseball is what, six months? Basketball, hockey; same thing. Limited. Wrestlers were there every week all year long. They became heroes, and people wanted to be the American Dream Dusty Rhodes and Superstar Billy Graham and Junkyard Dog. It was like you got to live your favorite comic-book character in real life or your favorite movie star. Ric Flair was your villain, and he came back every week. Women had All My Children. We had Saturday Night's Main Event, and it was a great part of American pop culture. It's an art in China. In Japan, it's one of the most respected art forms. In Mexico, it's tradition. And in Europe, they sing songs when their favorite wrestler comes out. When I hear people talk about it and say,

"Oh, it's fake," I roll my eyes. These same people, when they come out of Terminator, do they say, "Arnold Schwarzenegger is not really a robot"? Of course not.

Cowards love to bring down heroes. And right now, we live in a time where cowards, liars, and false prophets love to bring down anything that brings other people joy because it keeps the focus away from them. One of my biggest criticisms I hear is, "Why did you wear that damn belt?" Well, I'll be happy to tell you why. Because I'm the NWA Worlds Heavyweight Champion. Hopefully, by the time this book's out, I still am. If I'm not, I'm the former NWA Worlds Heavyweight Champion. And I was the Funkasaurus in the WWE. I get stopped to this day by people who, as kids, would jump up and dance in front of the TV just like I did when the American Dream came out and tell me how much it meant to them and how much they loved it and how much it inspired them. Wrestling is an American pastime. It's a cultural phenomenon. And if you don't like me wearing the belt on TV, I got four consonants for you: GFYS.

Pro wrestling is a way to forget our problems and lose ourselves in the excitement and drama of the ring. Say what you want about wrestling. For me, it helped save my life way back when, and it continues to do that today. It's a lot more work than most people are aware of, and we take our jobs seriously. Because we know that means something to a lot of people. For those of you who get it, we get you. I promise. We get you.

Nuff said.

CHAPTER 12

Term Limits

Time for some straight talk about term limits and age limits for politicians.

I know some of y'all might think this is some boring, wonky stuff, but let me tell you, it's anything but. This is about democracy, representation, and accountability. So, let's break it down and talk about why we need term limits and why old politicians need to step aside.

First off, let's talk about term limits. For those who don't know, term limits are restrictions on how long a politician can serve in office. Most countries, including the US, have some form of term limits, whether it's for the presidency, the legislature, or other elected offices. The idea behind term limits is simple: to prevent politicians from becoming too entrenched, too powerful, or too corrupt. By limiting their time in office, we can ensure that fresh ideas, new voices, and diverse perspectives can enter the political arena, and that the interests of the people, not just the interests of the politicians, are being served.

Now, some folks might argue that term limits are undemocratic, or that they deprive voters of their right to choose who they want to represent them. But let's be real here. Term limits are not a violation of democracy, they're a safeguard against it. Without term limits, politicians can become careerists, more interested in their own power and privilege than in serving the public. They can become beholden to special interests, lobbyists, or party bosses, rather than to the people who elected them. They can become complacent, disconnected, or out of touch with the needs and aspirations of their constituents. And they can become corrupt, using their office for personal gain instead of public service.

That's why we need term limits, y'all. We need to ensure that our democracy is vibrant, responsive, and accountable to the people, not just to the politicians. We need to prevent the accumulation of too much power or influence in the hands of a few and encourage the participation and engagement of many. We need to foster a culture of public service, where people enter politics not to enrich themselves, but to make a positive difference in the lives of others.

I hear people saying both parties suck. The parties don't suck. We got to stop electing people that suck. And we need term limits. We need to start saying, "Hey, Mitch, hey, Pelosi, you've been in this too long. We're not voting for you anymore. Sorry. You're out. You're not going to die on the job." You're not going to have people voting for you when you don't have the ability to feed yourself anymore. When you have to be wheeled into work with a wheelchair and it looks like you don't know the time of day, you should not be serving. It goes back to the fact that you are representing millions of people and if you're not at your best, you shouldn't be doing it.

Again, we need to stop voting for people we know can't do the job anymore.

I loved John McCain. I thought John McCain was an American hero. I thought he was a good senator. But there was no reason for him, when he was struggling with cancer, to stay in office. There's no other job where this is allowed. You work at the library and you can't do the job anymore, they're going to replace you. But you can still be a senator or congressman. Ridiculous.

The American people have to decide collectively to make changes. If politicians won't pass term limits themselves, you do it. We saw what happened when Americans got together and let Bud Light know they went too far with a trans influencer spokesperson.

Everything gets blamed on the president, but the president can't do his damn job when there are senators and congressmen who go out of their way to obstruct all the time. We saw it when Barack Obama was in office. Mitch McConnell had his little meeting at the Waffle House, they decided he was going to be a one-term president, and the whole basis was to steal a Supreme Court pick. Then President Trump gets in, and all the Democrats decide they're not only not going to work with him, they're going to impeach him and they're going to get him out with no real evidence, nothing to support their case other than "we know what's better for the American people." So what should have happened after the after all this stuff that's coming out with the FBI and the Clintons and all this stuff that was going on? Every person involved in that should ask to be voted out the next time their seat's up.

Until we're accountable, we suck because we're putting these dumbasses, these crooks back in office. If your family members are getting rich off Wall Street and you're sitting in the House, or in the Senate, you should be impeached immediately because you're using inside information to line your pockets at the expense of the American people.

The people suck because we vote lazy. The party system is the problem. It's lazy voting, and we all have to do a better job. There is no reason that Mitch McConnell, Chuck Schumer, Diane Feinstein, and others (as of this writing) should be in office for as long as they are. That's on us. That's lazy voting. Get it together. Vote these people out. Thank them for the service and move them on. Look at Bernie Sanders. Claims he is a socialist and wants everyone else to give up everything they have while he sits with two mansions. Utterly ridiculous. These giant book deals. They get these book deals that are based off lobbyists, giving guys million-dollar book deals and literally nothing about them is interesting at all, except the fact that they took dollars and they do whatever the special interests and lobbyists ask them to do. They kowtow. They bend down to every Black Lives Matter and George Soros-supported DA. Why? Not because they share their beliefs. Because they line their pockets. So we need to get our asses in gear. You can blame them all you want to, but then you vote for them. That makes zero sense. This is on us to change.

That's not all, folks. We also need to talk about age limits for politicians. Now, I know some of y'all might think this is ageism or discrimination, but hear me out. Age limits are not about excluding older people from politics or disrespecting their experience or wisdom. Age limits are about recognizing that politics is a demanding, complex, and rapidly changing field, and that not everyone, regardless of their age, can keep up with it.

Let's face it. Politics is not just about being old and wise. It's about being agile, adaptable, and innovative. It's about being able to navigate a complex web of issues, stakeholders, and challenges, and to come up with creative and effective solutions. It's about being able to communicate, collaborate, and lead, in a diverse and dynamic environment. And it's about being able to connect with the younger generations, who are shaping the future of our society and our planet.

That's why age limits are important, y'all. We need to ensure that our politicians are not just experienced, but also current, relevant, and connected to the needs and aspirations of today's world.

We need to prevent the stagnation, the resistance to change, and the lack of vision that can come with old age. We need to encourage a culture of innovation, where people of all ages can contribute their talents and ideas, and where the wisdom of the elders is balanced by the energy of the youth.

Of course, age limits should not be arbitrary or discriminatory. They should be based on objective criteria, such as cognitive abilities, physical health, and mental agility. They should be applied equally to all politicians, regardless of their party affiliation, gender, race, or socioeconomic status. And they should be accompanied by support and resources for older politicians who want to transition to other roles or activities, such as mentoring, teaching, or advocacy.

Term limits and age limits are not just theoretical concepts or abstract principles. They're practical measures that can make a real difference in the quality, effectiveness, and legitimacy of our political system. They can help prevent the abuses, the corruption, and the complacency that can come with too much power or too much age. They can ensure that our democracy is vibrant, responsive, and accountable to the people, not just to the politicians. And they can encourage a culture of public service, where people of all ages and backgrounds can contribute their talents and ideas for the common good. So, let's get real, y'all, and demand term limits and age limits for politicians. It's time to bring some fresh air, some new blood, and some real change to our political system.

𝔑𝔲𝔣𝔣 𝔖𝔞𝔦𝔡

The Two-Party System
Ain't Much of a Party

Democrats are supposed to be the "progressive" party, the ones who are all about social justice, equality, and all that good stuff. But let's be real here—they're just as corrupt and out of touch as everyone they criticize.

For starters, they're completely beholden to corporate interests. They talk a big game about fighting for the little guy, but when it comes down to it, they're more than happy to take money from big banks, pharmaceutical companies, and other corporate giants.

Don't even get me started on their pandering. They love to talk about diversity and inclusion, but when it comes time to actually do something about it, they fall short. They're more than happy to put a person of color or a woman in a high-profile position, but they're not willing to address the systemic issues that keep those same people from succeeding.

Republicans are not perfect either. These guys are supposed to be the party of small government, personal responsibility, and fiscal conservatism. But again, let's be real—often-times they are just as out of touch as the Democrats.

For starters, they're completely beholden to the wealthy elite. They talk a big game about cutting taxes and shrinking government, but when it comes down to it, they're more than happy to do the bidding of their wealthy donors.

They also love to talk about personal responsibility and family values, but when it comes time to actually live up to those ideals, they sometimes fall short. They're more than happy to preach abstinence-only education and oppose same-sex marriage, but they're not willing to address the real issues facing families and communities.

So, what's the problem here? Why can't either party get their act together? Well, there are a few reasons.

First of all, both parties are too focused on winning elections and maintaining power. They're more concerned with playing political games and scoring points against the other side than actually doing what's best for the country.

Secondly, both parties are too entrenched in their own ideologies. They're more concerned with sticking to their party line than listening to their constituents and working together to find solutions.

Finally, both parties are too reliant on big-money donors. As long as they're beholden to wealthy interests, they're never going to be able to truly represent the people they're supposed to be serving.

So what's the solution? How do we fix this mess? It's not going to be easy, but here are a few suggestions:

First, we need to break the stranglehold that the two major parties have on our political system. We need to encourage third-party candidates and give them a chance to be heard. We

Hustlers Gonna Hustle (Welcome to BLM)

Kerry, Al Gore, Bill Gates and countless other self-important, pompous blowhard celebrities travel the world holding climate summits with world leaders, politicians and other hypocritical elites, it becomes obvious very quickly what's going on. Just look at how they travel. Private jets, private jets, and more private jets. Carbon footprint? Whatever. These millionaires and even billionaires who are constantly telling us to get rid of our gas-powered stoves and gas-powered automobiles to go fully electric, even if no infrastructure is built for it, all need to be held accountable. I'm not sure that's going to happen anytime soon, but we can ignore them or even better, reject everything they say and stand for. Because they are phonies. When people like coal miners lose jobs thanks to their harebrained decisions, it doesn't affect them. They keep moving the goalposts though in terms of how much time we have left. Twenty years? Ten years? Go look at Al Gore's movie and tell me how right he was. Even better, tell me how wrong he was. It's just scare tactics designed to raise money so they can travel to the most exotic cities and eat at the best restaurants while attending their all-important climate summits.

No matter what they have been warning us about, the polar bears all seem to be in pretty good shape. Even the glaciers, at least according to some scientists, are getting stronger in Antarctica. Some species come and go. That's just the way of the world. I really don't think there's much we can do about the earth changing. And it's arrogant to say that we can. It's embarrassing.

If anyone's in trouble, it's people. We'll eat and breed ourselves out of room. We'll pollute ourselves, make it impossible for us to go on. But the planet will keep going. There are organisms on this planet that are just waiting for their turn to take over. Maybe it's the cockroach. Maybe he's going to get a run. It's just arrogant to constantly talk about how the planet is so fragile and only they can save it. That's complete bullshit and they know it, but they make money from it. It sounds good. They get awards for it. They get more money to buy private jets. They get TV specials, and they get to trash on regular old taxpayers who cannot afford an electric car that can only fit two people in it.

They are all, "I'm so virtuous. Just don't ask me to give anything up because I can't save the world if I don't have a private jet." Virtuousness is a first-world problem. They want to take down the oil companies because they want their money. It always comes down to money. And that's why it's always the rich who do it.

Whenever you see somebody patting himself on the back with one arm, you're going to notice the other one's reaching for your wallet. That's the way it works. Especially when it comes to climate-change activists. They are hustlers, plain and simple. You can be concerned about the planet. But when you start making demands on people and you are unwilling to give up any of your own elitist creature comforts, then I think you need to shut your fucking mouth.

The next big hustle? Black Lives Matter. BLM defines itself as a decentralized social justice movement that originated in the African American community. They like to claim they are not a traditional non-profit organization and are not required to disclose their financial information and that they have been transparent about how it uses its funding. I call BS. I know that many "social justice" movements, including BLM, rely on grassroots fundraising efforts to sustain their work. This means that individuals from the community donate money to support the cause. But who holds them accountable? BLM claims that the criticism directed at them may be driven by political or ideological differences; that the movement's outspokenness on issues such as police brutality and systemic racism has made it a target for criticism from those who disagree with its message or goals. Again, BS. BLM has *not* been transparent about how it uses its funding.

Here's the thing. BLM is a hustle. They're only concerned that Black lives matter as long as it's at the hands of a white cop or a white person doing bad something to a Black person. It's about making money. Lots of it. Because rich virtue-signaling white people will cut checks to clear their conscience. There's no money in Black-on-Black crime. Who's going to give you money for that? That's the reality of it. But Black Lives Matter.

It also bothers me sometimes when I hear people get so upset over Black Lives Matter. But look at your churches. Look at all these political groups that are supposedly for the people but are never really for the people. Look at every politician that owns a mansion. Was that for the people? It was for themselves. It's all the same. It's the American way. You create a monster that no one challenges and people give you checks for that monster. Black Lives Matter makes lots of money for its leaders and everyone is too scared to argue with them. Everyone took a knee for BLM. Everyone wanted to talk to them. Every police chief wanted to march with them. There was a concerted effort from law enforcement, from politicians, from donors, from celebrities. Everybody wanted to be part of Black Lives Matter.

The only thing that Black Lives Matter cared about was to make sure that white cops weren't allowed to be on the force anymore. All they cared about was getting money from George Soros and other white people, which is ironic because it's the money coming from white people that allows them to go after more white people. That in itself is the point.

Black Lives Matter has nothing to do with Black people, and it has nothing to do with white people. It has to do with the group of individuals who put this hustle together. It always starts the same way. It's always like this with every crooked charity. They want to do so much to help the people until they realize that it takes actual work. They get money and what's the first thing they do? They buy mansions, they buy planes, and they give all their relatives jobs. It's the same thing we see in politics. Same thing we see with religious groups. When you donate money to these charities that are supposed to help these victims, do you ever look to see where the money goes? How much of it actually goes to the person or persons in trouble? Do you ever wonder why when you see a commercial for these groups, to help a dog or help a hospital with cancer-ridden children, say "If you do this today, we'll give you this wonderful blanket?" How much does that blanket cost? Keep the blanket. Use every dime to go to fight cancer or to put towards the children. Because this is the hustle. These are the charity hustles, and Black Lives Matter has opened the same playbook. The difference is, they've got every media camera on them, and everybody wants to be down with Black Lives Matter. But no one ever bothered to check the content and character of those doing it. They never saw them rebuild a building that was burnt down with all the money they made or purchase laptop computers for all the children in the lower socioeconomic groups and schools. As I'm writing this, according to public documents, Black Lives Matter donated a little over $30 million, or 33 percent of the roughly $90 million in public donations it collected between 2020 and 2022, to charitable foundations. According to two federal filings that cover the time period from July 1, 2020, to June 30, 2022, the Oakland, California-based Black Lives Matter Global Network Foundation donated the $30,498,722 in donations to black, trans, and anti-police non-profits in the fiscal years for 2020 and 2021. Even though BLMGNF reported losses of more than $8.5 million last year, its most recent public filings for the fiscal year 2021 show that the organization gave $4.5 million to non-profits run by the movement's own supporters and friends.

Compare them to Nipsey Hussle, the rapper who was on the brink of becoming an international star. He was often compared to Snoop because he was skinny, but he was very different. Like Snoop, though, Nipsey was about giving it back to the people. He was about his STEM (Science, Technology, Engineering, Math) program that helped empower his community.

That's how Black lives mattered to him. His whole focus was trying to raise money to build his neighborhoods up. That's a hero. That's somebody that I would gladly cut a check to or put in time and help out. Snoop with his work with his youth football league gives not just to Black kids, but Hispanic kids, white kids; anybody on a lower socioeconomic level. He gives them all a chance. It doesn't mean that it's a road to the NFL. It's a road to be a part of a team. It's a road to make friends, build relationships, and have help in school. That's the true Black Lives Matter.

BLM was a hustle from the jump. When the George Floyd shit happened, every first-world virtue signaler cut a check to

Black Lives Matter and got fleeced. Overnight, they became powerful. They had the money to back it up and everybody was taking a knee to them, literally. It became fashionable. Because here's the thing. It's not the color of skin. It's character, man. And we keep falling for this shit. Black Lives Matter was a hustle just like every other hustle.

Another big hustle today? The concept of reparations to Black people.

The issue of reparations for Black Americans is a highly controversial concept that has been debated for decades after the topic was reignited in the 1980s. The idea of reparations is rooted in the history of slavery and its legacy, which has had a profound impact on the lives of Black Americans. Liberals who support reparations argue that they are necessary to address this historical and ongoing harm, while opponents (*me*) argue that they are impractical or unworkable. Or just plain stupid.

One of the main arguments in favor of reparations is that they are necessary to address the historical and ongoing harm done to Black Americans through centuries of slavery, segregation, and discrimination. The legacy of slavery is still felt today in the form of racial disparities in wealth, health, education, and the criminal justice system. According to a recent study by the Brookings Institution, the median wealth of white households is ten times greater than that of Black households, and the average white family has seven times more wealth than the average Black family. These disparities are not just the result of individual choices or behaviors but are rooted in a history of institutional racism and discrimination. I get that. But so what? Nobody alive today had anything to do with this.

Liberals argue that they could help address these disparities and create a more equitable society. They argue that reparations could take many forms, such as direct payments to Black Americans, investments in education and job training programs, or the creation of policies that address systemic racism. They argue that reparations are not just a matter of justice, but also a matter of economic and social policy.

But how could you possibly implement any of this fairly and effectively? It's never made clear who would be eligible for reparations, and how much they would receive. Some argue that reparations should only be given to those who can prove a direct link to slavery, while others argue that all Black Americans should receive some form of compensation. It is also not clear how much reparations would cost, and who would pay for them. Some argue that the government should foot the bill, while others argue that private companies that profited from slavery should contribute.

Reparations are also unfair to those who did not benefit from slavery. Many white Americans today are the descendants of immigrants who arrived in the United States after slavery was abolished and did not benefit from the wealth and privilege that slavery provided to earlier generations.

Reparations would also perpetuate a victim mentality and actually harm race relations by creating a sense of entitlement among Black Americans and perpetuating a narrative of Black victimization. This, in turn, would create resentment among white Americans who feel that they are being unfairly blamed for the actions of their ancestors. So it actually would make race relations worse, rather than better.

I'll tell you why. First of all, reparations originally were never about money. Reparations were about opportunity.

At the time, the biggest companies were farms. If you had acres and a mule, you could plant seeds, build wealth, and pass a legacy down to your family. Because everyone was farming, whether it was cotton, corn, tobacco, alfalfa, or hay, you could turn that around in one summer. You could turn your entire life around. Reparations were about allowing former slaves onto the same playing field as other Americans, as migrants coming in. It wasn't supposed to put you in first class. It was supposed to allow you through the door to give you a chance in the race. Of course, like everything else today with these first-world problems, it all is manipulated. You want to give reparations to a group of people. And here's the frustrating thing about being African American. We don't necessarily have roots. You have to do a DNA check to find out where you came from, and then you find out what tribe you originated from, whether you were African or West Indian. Whatever your origin, you can't go back to that tribe. You can't go back to that country because you're different. You don't speak the language. You don't know the customs. You're American. So you are starting from where your family came from. A lot of us didn't get shit passed down to us. All I got passed down to me was DNA. But, luckily, I was born in the United States, where you can go from zero to a hero. You don't necessarily know who was a slave because there are little or no records. And, of course, not all Blacks were slaves. Some even owned slaves. Because when you had money and wealth in the United States, you had slaves to do your work. There was a decent-sized population of Blacks that owned slaves. So do they get the money? Or what about the Englishmen who gave their lives fighting to stop slavery in Africa? Where do you draw the line with reparations?

Reparations in this country are called opportunity. That's how I look at it. I'm not looking for handouts.

I would much rather do things myself, because when you take handouts, you become dependent on whoever gave you that handout. Reparations would be just more welfare. It will simply make people dependent on the system. We all know what free money does to society. It corrupts people and makes them lazy and unmotivated. It's never any good. In this country, you have to earn it. The only people who want free money are the same people who were scamming during the pandemic and the same people who want to have kids for profit. What I mean by that is they want to get child support. The irony is, of course—they are basically enslaving themselves to the people giving them the money. Earning it is always better. That person working at McDonald's is going to work their way up. Maybe they will become a manager and then maybe someday they will own their own franchise. Or maybe McDonald's was just a stepping stone to help pay for junior college classes. Whatever the stories, that person is getting off their ass and trying to earn something the right way. All I have ever wanted in this country is an opportunity to pursue my passion. I've done my best, and with a lot of failures. But I never stopped. I never stopped working hard nor will I ever stop working hard.

If the state of California called me today and offered me reparations because they figured out that my great-great-grandparents were slaves, I would refuse the money. I would tell them I work for my living. I think most of us feel that way. We don't want free money. We want opportunity. We want the freedom to pursue our happiness. We want the ability to go to sleep at night without having to worry about somebody kicking in our door trying to hustle us and scam us and steal our money. That's not a Black thing. That's a people thing. I've always had a problem with free rides.

When I first went to kindergarten, snack was milk and graham crackers. At lunchtime, you would get your tray, go down the line and they would scoop your little lasagna or whatever to your plate. Then you would get milk or chocolate milk if there was any chocolate left. That was always a lucky day when they had not yet run out of chocolate milk. But you couldn't take your lunch to the table and eat unless you gave them a lunch ticket, which were sent home in the mail.

One day, I forgot my ticket. The teacher helping out at the register asked me for it, and I told her I had forgotten it at home. She nicely said to me, "It's okay, come with me." She took my hand and walked me over to a cafeteria worker who said, "It's okay, I think he's on the free lunch program. He doesn't need a ticket." I knew that wasn't true. "I don't want a free lunch. I have lunch tickets at home," I told her. Even at that young age, I would rather have gone without than get something for nothing. I was fundamentally against it. I would just wait until snack time later in the day. The teacher, who was being nice, was not my everyday teacher and I think she just assumed because I was Black, I was part of the free lunch program. I didn't want to be treated like that. But she wasn't helping me with that attitude. If she really wanted to help me, she could have lent me the money to get lunch, I would've told my mom, and the next day at school I would've brought the money and paid her back. I'm not sure why I was like that at such a young age, but I was. I've never had a welfare mentality. Also, keep in mind, there's no such thing as free. When someone gives you something like that, they're telling you you're not able to do it yourself. I know there are times when people need help. I'm not stupid about that. But that's not what I'm talking about. I'm talking about a system that rewards people for doing nothing, not an emergency situation. I will never understand or accept that.

Another example that was set for me when I was young took place when I would visit my biological grandmother. My birth dad's mother. That house was full of people. Eight adults and a bunch of children. Nobody was doing well. Just a series of close friends and distant relatives. And what would my grandmother do? The first of the month she'd get dressed up and go down to the post office. She would bring everyone with her and line them up for welfare checks. She was a master at filling out the paperwork that enabled all of them to get their handouts. I could not believe that. And I couldn't stand it. That never seemed right to me. That welfare statement tally. That slave mentality. In its own way, the welfare state is another big hustle whereby people who need help are used as pawns by those in charge. The welfare system isn't designed to help them succeed, it is designed to make them become reliant on the government. Just like the way climate change is. Just like the way Black Lives Matter wants everyone to fall in line and become reliant on whatever bullshit they happen to be pushing. These are all hustles. And they are all designed to take away your freedom and basically make you a ward of the state.

Listen up, the government handing out freebies left and right is like giving a kid unlimited access to the candy aisle. It might seem sweet at first, but it's gonna rot your teeth and make you sick in the long run.

Now, don't get me wrong, I'm not saying we shouldn't help people who are struggling. But when you're just handing out cash like it's Halloween candy, you're creating a culture of dependency. People start thinking they don't need to work for anything because the government's got their back. And that's a problem, because when you're not working, you're not contributing to society. You're not paying taxes, you're not creating value, you're not building anything. You're just sitting on your butt, waiting for the next handout to come along.

That's a dangerous mindset to have. Because when you're not contributing, you're not invested in the success of the country. You don't care about the future, because you're not building it. And that's how you get a generation of entitled, lazy, ungrateful people who think the world owes them something.

Now, some folks will say, "But Tyrus, what about the people who really need help? What about the homeless, or the disabled, or the elderly?" To them I say, fair point. We should help those who truly can't help themselves. But that's not what we're talking about here.

We're talking about able-bodied adults who are perfectly capable of working but choose not to. We're talking about people who would rather leech off the government than put in an honest day's work. And that's just not right. When you're given something for nothing, you don't appreciate it. You don't understand the value of hard work, because you've never had to do it. And that's how you get a bunch of entitled moochers who think they're owed something just for existing.

And let's be real here, folks. There's no such thing as a free lunch. Somebody's gotta pay for all these handouts, and it's usually the hardworking taxpayers who are footing the bill. So while you might get a temporary boost from a government handout, in the long run you're just creating more problems than you're solving. So let's stop pretending that giving people free handouts is some kind of magic solution to poverty.

It's not. It's just a Band-Aid on a much deeper problem. If we really want to help people, we need to focus on creating jobs, building up our economy, and teaching people the value of hard work.

In the end, it's the people who work hard and contribute to society who are gonna come out on top. The rest of you can keep waiting for your next government handout, but don't be surprised when the candy store runs out of treats.

'Nuff Said

Hold China Accountable

While I was writing this book, the US Energy Department concluded that the COVID pandemic most likely arose from a laboratory leak. Duh. Please don't tell me any of y'all still believe the bat story. Come on, people.

China needs to be held accountable for the COVID pandemic because it's caused an unprecedented amount of death, suffering, and economic turmoil around the world. This isn't some small-potatoes issue that we can brush under the rug and move on from. We need to figure out what went wrong, where things could have been done better, and how we can prevent something like this from happening again.

Now, let's talk about this bat excuse. Look, I get it, bats are weird and scary, and they carry all sorts of diseases. But blaming the COVID pandemic on some poor little bat is like blaming a fart on the dog. It's a convenient scapegoat that allows people to deflect responsibility and avoid accountability.

The truth is, we don't know exactly how COVID started. There are theories and hypotheses and a lot of scientific investigations going on, but still no definitive answers. What we do know is that the virus emerged in Wuhan, China, and quickly spread around the world. We also know that there were some serious missteps and cover-ups on the part of Chinese officials early on, which likely contributed to the virus's rapid spread.

But blaming it all on bats? Come on. That's like saying the Titanic sank because of an iceberg. Sure, the iceberg played a role, but there were a whole lot of other factors at play too.

So why is the bat excuse so ridiculous? For one thing, it's based on a pretty flimsy piece of evidence. There was a market in Wuhan that sold live animals, including bats, and some early cases of COVID were traced back to people who had visited the market. But that doesn't necessarily mean that the virus originated from bats. It could have been passed from another animal to humans, or it could have been circulating in the community before the market outbreak.

Furthermore, blaming the pandemic on bats ignores the larger systemic issues that contributed to its spread. Things like inadequate public health infrastructure, lack of preparedness for a global pandemic, and misinformation and conspiracy theories that fueled mistrust and confusion.

But hey, let's say for argument's sake that it is true. Let's say some guy did eat a bat and that's how the virus started. That still doesn't excuse China's response to the situation. They knew about the virus back in December of 2019, and what did they do? Did they warn the rest of the world? Did they take action to contain the virus? No, they did nothing. They let it spread unchecked, and now we're all paying the price.

They silenced doctors who tried to speak out. They denied that the virus could be transmitted from human to human.

They even went so far as to accuse the United States of creating the virus and spreading it in China.

But we all know the truth. China is responsible for this pandemic, and they need to be held accountable. They need to pay for the lives that have been lost, the economies that have been destroyed, and the pain that has been inflicted on the world.

And it's not just about justice, folks. It's about preventing this from happening again. We need to send a message to China that this kind of behavior will not be tolerated. We need to make it clear that the world will hold them accountable for their actions.

Now, I know some of you out there might be saying, "But how do we do that? How do we hold China accountable?" Well, there are a few things we can do.

First, we need to demand an independent investigation into the origins of the virus. We need to find out exactly what happened in Wuhan and who is responsible. And if it turns out that China was responsible, then they need to be held accountable.

Second, we need to impose sanctions on China. We need to hit them where it hurts: in their wallets. We need to make it clear that there will be consequences for their actions.

And third, we need to stop relying on China for our goods. We need to bring manufacturing back to the United States and other countries. We need to stop relying on China for everything from pharmaceuticals to electronics.

Now, I know that's easier said than done. But we need to start somewhere. We need to take action to ensure that this kind of thing never happens again.

Summing it up for the slow folks that blame wet markets and bats: China needs to be held accountable for COVID. They need to pay for their actions, and they need to know that the world will not stand for this kind of behavior. We need to demand an independent investigation, impose sanctions, and stop relying on China for our goods.

It's time to take a stand, folks. It's time to hold China accountable for what they've done. And if they don't like it, tough luck. Because we're not going to let them get away with it.

Nuff said.

CHAPTER 14

R-E-S-P-E-C-T

Parenting is tough. We all know that. I always work hard to be the best dad I can be, but, of course, I fail sometimes. We all do. But we try hard as we can. I keep my life with my kids private, but it doesn't mean that I can't share some of the things I believe go into being a good parent.

The main thing is teaching your kids respect. Sadly, we are watching parts of society crumble today due to the simple fact that many young people are not being taught by their parents the basic rules of respect. That's why I wanted to take some time here to lay out what I see as one of the most essential principles. Look, I'm not a perfect parent. Far from it. I'm a work in progress. I'm always learning. But I'm trying. Teaching kids respect is something I try to get better at every day. When I go speak to kids in school, it's one of the main points I hit. So allow me to share some of the things I've learned over the years.

Respect is an essential value that every parent wants their child to learn. It is not only a crucial component of healthy relationships, it also helps children become responsible, empathetic, and compassionate individuals. Teaching children respect is a continuous process that requires patience, consistency, and positive reinforcement. In my opinion, these are a few effective strategies that all parents can use to raise their kids. Let's just call it:

Tyrus's top 10 list of what to teach your kids.

1. Be a Good Role Model—this is basic 101!

    Children learn by observing and imitating their parents. Therefore, one of the most effective ways to teach children respect is by modeling respectful behavior yourself. Children who see their parents showing respect to others are more likely to do the same. Here are some ways you can model respectful behavior:

    - Respect your child's feelings, opinions, and ideas, even if you do not agree with them.
    - Speak politely and kindly to your child, and use respectful language.
    - Show respect to other family members, friends, and strangers, even when you disagree with them.
    - Avoid using negative or derogatory language when talking about others, especially in front of your child.
    - Apologize when you make a mistake and ask for forgiveness when you hurt someone's feelings.

2. Set Clear Expectations—it's not always easy, but you have to do it!

Children need to know what is expected of them regarding respectful behavior. Parents should set clear boundaries and expectations around how children should treat others. Here are some ways you can set clear expectations:

- Explain what respect means and why it is essential.
- Discuss what behaviors are acceptable and unacceptable in your family.
- Encourage them to speak respectfully to others and avoid using hurtful language.
- Teach them to listen actively and pay attention when others are talking.
- Show them how to show appreciation to others and express gratitude.

3. Praise Respectful Behavior—we all want validation, don't forget how it makes you feel!

Children respond well to positive reinforcement. Parents should praise their children when they show respectful behavior. Here are some ways you can praise respectful behavior:

- Show them how proud you are when they show respect to others.
- Use positive reinforcement, such as a high-five, hug, or praise to reward respectful behavior.
- Acknowledge their effort to change their behavior and show respect to others.

- Encourage them to continue to behave respectfully by praising their efforts consistently.

4. Use a Respectful Tone—they will respect you back.

I'll admit, I sometimes slip on this one, but I always think about it.

The tone of voice a parent uses when talking to
their child impacts how they respond, so it is
essential to use a respectful tone when speaking
to them. Here are four easy tips:

- Speak calmly and avoid yelling or using a harsh
tone.
- Use a tone that expresses kindness and compassion.
- Listen and acknowledge their feelings and
needs.
- Avoid interrupting them when they are speaking to you. Let them finish.

5. Encourage Empathy—in today's me-me-me-me
world, this one often gets left aside, but it's critical.

Empathy is the ability to understand and share the
feelings of others. It is an essential skill that helps
children show respect to others. Here are some
ways you can encourage empathy in your child:

- Encourage your child to put themselves in
other people's shoes and imagine how they
would feel in a similar situation.

- Teach your child to listen actively and pay attention when others are talking.
- Help your child identify and express their emotions and feelings.
- Encourage your child to be kind and compassionate to others.

6. Teach Conflict Resolution Skills—yes, I've been in a few fights, but I have learned the importance of conflict resolution as well.

   Conflict is a natural part of relationships. It is essential to teach children how to resolve conflicts in a respectful manner. Here are some ways you can teach conflict resolution skills:

   - Teach your child how to express their feelings and needs without being disrespectful or hurtful to others.
   - Encourage your child to use "I" statements when expressing their feelings, such as "I feel upset when you do that."
   - Teach your child to listen actively and try to understand the other person's perspective.
   - Help your child find a solution that works for everyone involved.
   - Model respectful conflict resolution skills yourself.

7. Use Consequences for Disrespectful Behavior— aka "punishment." It's okay to punish!

When children behave disrespectfully, it is essential to use consequences to help them learn from their mistakes. Here are some ways you can use consequences for disrespectful behavior:

- Explain to your child why their behavior was disrespectful and how it affected others.
- Set clear consequences for disrespectful behavior, such as losing privileges, having a time-out, or apologizing.
- Follow through with consequences consistently.
- Use consequences as an opportunity to teach your child about respect and how to behave respectfully in the future.

8. Teach Respect for Diversity—now more important than ever.

The world becomes a little bit different every day, lots of different kinds of people, and it's important to be inclusive, just make sure it's based on character and not some sort of virtue-signaling, patronizing attitude.

Respect for diversity means acknowledging and celebrating differences in people, such as race, ethnicity, religion, and culture. Teaching respect for diversity is essential in raising children who are tolerant and accepting of others. Here are some ways you can teach respect for diversity:

- Expose your child to people from different backgrounds and cultures.

- Encourage your child to ask questions and learn about different cultures and religions.
- Teach your child to show respect for different beliefs and customs.
- Model respectful behavior towards people from different backgrounds.

9. Encourage Independence—even if it hurts.

There are too many helicopter parents these days. Learning how to cut the strings is just as important as learning how to tie them together at the beginning. You will survive this, people, I promise. Do a good job upfront so that you have nothing to worry about.

Encouraging independence in children can help them develop a sense of responsibility and respect for themselves and others. Here are some ways you can encourage independence:

- Teach your child age-appropriate skills, such as dressing themselves, preparing simple meals, and doing household chores.
- Give your child opportunities to make decisions and solve problems independently.
- Praise your child's efforts and accomplishments, even if they do not succeed.
- Encourage your child to take responsibility for their actions and make amends when they make mistakes.

10. Practice Active Listening—it's becoming a lost art.

Have I always been a good listener? No. Have my kids taught me how to be a better listener? A hundred percent.

Active listening is an important skill that helps children show respect to others. Here are some ways you can practice active listening with your child:

- Pay attention when your child is talking to you and avoid distractions.
- Try to understand your child's perspective and feelings.
- Ask questions to clarify your child's thoughts and feelings.
- Reflect back what your child has said to show that you have understood them.

Okay, so that's my top 10 list of ways that you can instill respect in your kids. I am far from being a perfect parent, but I take it more seriously than anything else in my life. I didn't have the best role models going up, but I have always tried to self-educate and learn from people around me that I respect as parents.

One little thing I left out. When I look at the younger generation today, in general I described them as being like soft grapes at room temperature. They don't seem to be able to handle a lot and they certainly have lost a lot of respect for people around them. I think a lot of that comes from the fact that parents try to be friends with their kids. Remember, it's a benevolent dictatorship at home. You are the boss. Your child is not your peer. You can have friends in your life, but they don't need to be your kids. That's not what parenting is about.

When I was growing up, my mother did the best she could. She did lots of things right but also did a lot of things wrong. But one thing she definitely got right was the understanding that kids need to experience three basic things as they grow up: pain, loss, and failure. It's hard to watch kids go through those things. But it's necessary. Sometimes they are going to have to cry. Sometimes they're going to have to experience loss. Sometimes they're going to have to be made fun of. Sometimes they're going to have to be corrected. That's a given. Not as their friends, but as their parents.

I remember something vividly. To begin with, my younger brother and I had a lot of issues growing up and, looking back on it, I think it had to do with a certain jealousy that my brother had of me. I'm not really sure where that came from because I was the one who was always in trouble and the one who was always being made fun of and the one that was getting hammered by our mom's boyfriend. Then again, I could hold my own, I didn't take any shit from anybody, and so maybe that's why he was jealous. I possessed certain survival skills that he seemed to be lacking.

But he definitely had it easier than me being the "good son." He would even join in when I would get punished. When I was about to get a spanking from my mother, she would tell him to go get a stick in the backyard, and he would be more than happy to go fetch. He could also be kind of sneaky, come to think about it, manipulating certain situations to make it appear as if I had been in the wrong when in fact it was him. But because he was the "good son" he always got the benefit of the doubt. I had done little to earn that kind of respect.

Well, to my mother's credit, I remember when I discovered just how aware she was of my brother's behavior.

She was no dummy, my mother. I think once she realized that he was manipulating me, she started to put together that he was manipulating her and Craig as well. My brother was crafty, I will give him that. But on one particular occasion, it blew up in his face. He and I were sitting on the couch playing a Sega Genesis game, *Madden*. Often times when we played video games, he would try and cheat me. We had a rule, especially playing this particular game. If you were at fourth down with five yards to go, you had to punt. I think most kids who played *Madden* will agree or relate to that rule. When it's fourth and five, you punt. You don't get to just throw it up in the air and get a first down because chances are, you probably will. It was a respected rule. And so when it was fourth and four, I punted it to him. He got the ball but quickly threw an interception. I ran it in for a touchdown and kicked the ball back to him. Soon, it's fourth and five for him, but he's not punting.

I was like, "Yo, what are you doing? Fourth and five. You got to punt."

"No, I don't have to."

"You *do* have to."

We continued arguing. I was saying, "Bro, you're cheating."

He said, "I don't have to do what you tell me to do."

He wanted to go for it. So he went for it and I picked him off again. This time when I picked him off, instead of just running in the end zone, I was zigzagging, eating up the clock. I was going to run the game out. As I was scoring the touchdown, he grabbed the Sega Genesis, smashed me in the face with it, and it busted open my lip.

My lip was bleeding everywhere. I was going to destroy him as a human being. He took off running down the hall. I'm coming down after him with a bloody lip. Now, up to this point in our life, every time that I tried to put my hands on him, my mom would step in and tell me to leave him alone. So he ran right to her like he always did. My mother looked at him and looked at me. She saw my lips bleeding. My brother was crowing, "He's trying to beat me up. He's trying to attack me!" I'm the one bleeding and he's the one yelling. My mother calmly asked what happened and I explained the situation. She paused a beat, looked at me, and said without blinking, "Just not in the house, okay?"

The look on my brother's face was like, *How could you?* And she's looking like, "You've gotten away with it for a long time, but you need to pay the bill today." I don't know if she was in a particularly good mood or whatever, but if you've ever seen the Grinch's grin, that was mine. I dragged him by his face down the steps out in the backyard to where he was about to pay for all the manipulation, all the stuff he was doing now. Unbeknownst to me, my mother had said to my brother, "I had warned you several times about messing with your brother." So now she was going to teach him a lesson. Or rather, I was.

I dragged him and dumped him out the door and told him to get up. My brother got up and as I balled my fist up because I was going to punch him in the face—he'd bloodied my lip and I was going to bloody his lip—the dude then tried to faint. He fainted like anyone you've ever seen in a movie. He rolled his eyes and fell forward. As he hit the ground, I said, "You idiot. No one falls forward when they faint."

I picked him up. I guess I was in a forgiving mood because I just punched him in the stomach as hard as I could, which took all the air out of him. As he squealed and cried on the ground, I had second thoughts that since he bloodied my lip that he needed to pay the same price. But then my mother came out and said to me, "He's done, leave him alone." Turning to my brother on the ground she said, "When are you going to realize your brother is a foot taller than you? When are you going to stop messing with him? It was time for you to pay your bill, and that's what happened today. But the next time you do something like this to him I'm not going to stop him."

My mother taught my brother a hard lesson that day about pain and suffering and responsibility along with some accountability. Also that there are consequences to actions. Shortly after this incident came to a close my mom came into my room and spoke privately with me.

"Hitting somebody half your size, with your size and your strength, you're going to hurt somebody. And I know he hit you in the face, bloodied your lip. But did he really hurt you? I let you teach him a lesson this time. And I'm proud that you didn't hit him in the face because you would have given him a black eye. You would have knocked his tooth out. You hit him in the stomach. But that's not how you're going to solve your problems. You're too big. People are going to go at you. They're going to go at you the rest of your life. You know why? Because they know they can. And as long as they can go at you, you're going to have this problem. Now, you beat him up. If you do this to someone at school, all they're going to see is this giant monster hitting somebody smaller than him. You're going to end up in jail. You're going to end up shot. I know your lip hurts and you're mad and he broke your game.

But violence is not going to solve anything. So, you're not hitting your brother again. The next time he does it, you need to come to me way before it happens. Because you're too big. You can't just fight people. You're just physically too strong."

I was thinking to myself, *Can you give this speech to Craig?* But I didn't. I just sat there and said, "Yes, ma'am." And I didn't hit my brother again after that.

My mother taught me two lessons that day. Obviously, I was on the better side of it, but at the same time, I also now had to find other ways to deal with my anger when someone did me wrong. In this case, my brother smashed me in the face with a Sega, and I thought the only way to deal with it was to beat him up. But my mother was trying to explain to me that I can't solve my problems that way. I can't hit him because I'm big and it didn't seem fair. But, as I learned, life's not fair. I never forgot how my mom taught me that the rules would be different for most of my life. Because of my size and strength, I couldn't retaliate the way most people could and should. I had to monitor myself because I could seriously put somebody in the hospital, or worse. That was a hard lesson for me to accept, at least back then. But I appreciate the fact that my mom wasn't afraid to take a hard stand and let me get at least one retaliatory shot back at my brother. That's some serious tough love right there. And it all ties back to those ten points I listed earlier about how to curate respect from your kids. It's never easy. Parenting is arguably the hardest thing in the world. But we make it even harder if we don't accept our role as parents and disciplinarians. Even when the decisions seem exceptionally difficult.

CHAPTER 15

𝔐𝔶 𝔉𝔬𝔵 𝔉𝔞𝔪𝔦𝔩𝔶

One of the things that is so cool about Fox News is how they allow you to promote different events and appearances you have coming up. Whether I'm on *Gutfeld!* or *The Five*, they'll give you a minute to mention a special show or book signing. Fox is smart about that. Even if they're not involved in the event, they know that if your name and reputation is growing out there, Fox News is the ultimate beneficiary. Everybody wins. It's all good.

While I was in the middle of writing this book, I had a stand-up show coming up in New Jersey that I mentioned on *The Five*, just like I have done plenty of other times in the past. But this situation became a little different. Usually, I'm mentioning appearances in pretty far-flung places around the country, but this one was a lot closer to where everyone at Fox works and lives, and Dana Perino looked at me and said, "Oh, I want to go!"

Now, I have to be honest. As I'll get into a little bit later, I don't think there's a more sincere, professional, stand-up human on the planet than Dana Perino. She just is what she is. But whenever someone expresses interest in coming to a show, at least in my experience as a performer—even when I was working as a bodyguard for Snoop Dogg—I figure their saying they want to attend is just an entertainment thing. You know, we all have "entertainment friends" who like to express interest in what we're doing. Whether or not they show up is not even the point. They want you to know they're thinking about you, and that's cool. You hear these things all the time. You bump into somebody out on the street and it becomes, "Oh, we have to get together!" But you both know you're not going to get together. It's just something you say; it's polite banter that has a ring of sincerity to it. That's just the way it is in the entertainment business. It's not good or bad—it just is.

But Dana is different. She doesn't just throw things out there. If she says something, she means it. So, in my head, even though a little part of me thought, *Oh, it's cool she's saying that*, I was also pretty sure that she was going to show up.

What I didn't expect a few minutes later was when Megan came over to me and said that she also wanted to go to the show. Megan Albano is Vice President of Weekend Primetime and *The Five*, and the person I truly consider to be my day-to-day boss—because she is! She's been supportive since I first walked in the door. Megan was the first to push me to get a shot on *The Five*, and then into the rotation. Most recently, she handpicked me to open up the new Saturday night show. I can always go to her for advice and to pitch ideas. She's a great leader in that she doesn't come off as a traditional boss. She wants to know what you think and how you feel about things, and she factors all of that into her decisions and into the programming. She's great at providing constructive criticism, too. She tells you when you've gone too far or when you haven't gone far enough. It's hard to put into words how much she's helped me grow and how much I hope she continues to help me grow in the future.

When Megan told me she wanted to come, I felt that shit was getting real. Megan seemed as serious as Dana did. Shortly after that, Judge Jeanine's assistant gave me a call and said, "Hey, the Judge would like to go to your show, too." Right after that, Suzanne Scott expressed interest. Now, you should know who she is. She's the head of Fox News and she's a badass.

Well now, I started thinking to myself, *this show better be really good*. I mean, I try to make every show great, but there are certain nights when you have to step it up. This was feeling like one of those nights. Normally, I'm not crazy about giving comp tickets away, for no other reason than when someone buys a ticket, they respect the ticket and you know they're going to show up. A lot of times with comp tickets, people will call you with all of these extra needs and requests—"Can I add another person?"—or they call you hours before the performance and say their friend can't make it, or can they change their seats, or one million other things. Comp tickets are usually a big pain in the ass. These comp tickets, though, were actually starting to feel pretty special.

I respected these women as much as anyone I've ever respected in my life. In numerous ways, they've all changed my life for the better. And now they want to come see me perform live? I look up to these people. It's a feeling beyond respect. I genuinely admire them, and—if we're being totally honest—I get a little bit intimidated around them because they're all so good at what they do.

On the day of the show, they all arrived early. Looking out from behind the curtain, I could see them in their seats. The crowd was buzzing, with many in the audience walking over to say hello to them. They were all incredibly generous with the crowd—waving, smiling, and shaking hands. Their presence added a certain excitement and energy to the show, and it inspired me to be my best.

The show was great and they all really seemed to enjoy it. I even directed a joke toward each one of them, which I think they appreciated. Afterward, they all came up onstage to take pictures together, and I have to say, that was a life-changing moment for me. In that single second up on the stage posing with them, I thought to myself, *I finally have a group of people who believe in me.* This was a moment. I was part of something. I'd always felt like I was part of something to some degree, but not like this. The fact that they all showed up and enjoyed themselves made me feel something even deeper.

They had faith in me. They took time out of their busy lives to come spend time watching a big goofball on stage. I know the word "family" gets overused when it comes to workplace environments, and maybe it's not even appropriate to use. I mean, do you really want to work with your family? But there is part of it that matters and that is perfectly appropriate for the workplace. To love the people you work with, to learn from the people you work with and to feel safe with the people you work with, definitely has a family feeling to it. And I really love that. It's something I've never felt before. As I sit here writing this book right now at this point in my life, I realize things are dramatically different for me. I owe a lot of that to the people I've gotten to know and work with at Fox News.

When I first got started in this business, I never could've imagined that I'd end up where I am today...working alongside some of the most talented and dedicated people in the industry.

One of the things that's always impressed me about Fox News is the level of professionalism and expertise that's on display every single day. From the producers to the reporters to the anchors, everyone here is dedicated to delivering the news with accuracy, integrity, and a commitment to excellence that's truly inspiring. But what really sets Fox News apart, in my mind, is the sense of camaraderie and mutual support that exists among the staff. Despite the long hours and high-pressure environment, everyone here is always willing to lend a hand, to share their knowledge and experience, and to work together.

That's why I'm so excited to let you all in on a little secret: behind the scenes at Fox News, we're more than just colleagues—we're a family. We work hard, we play hard, and we're there for each other through the good times and the bad. It's all about the people. From the top down, this network is filled with some of the most talented, passionate, and dedicated individuals I've ever had the pleasure of working with.

I had to build the house once I got into Fox News, but Greg Gutfeld opened the door. Right from the beginning, Greg had a way of communicating with me that made sense. He would look at things from angles I wasn't seeing. I always appreciated the fact that he forced me to look at things in different ways. Greg began his career as a writer and an editor, working for various magazines including *Men's Health*, then later became the editor-in-chief of the magazines *Stuff* and *Maxim*, where he gained a reputation for his irreverent and often controversial approach to editorial content. Those were the things that set the table for him at the network. Now he's one of the main faces of Fox News and a bestselling author.

Everything started when Greg and I exchanged a couple of tweets. I was invited onto the show, and the rest is history. Today, after all these years, I still gain valuable insights from him. If something is bothering me and I want to say something, he'll slow me down and encourage me to be patient. He'll get me to think about *why* something is upsetting me, which is very important. Very few people have that ability with me, but Greg definitely does.

Believe it or not, I think Greg would make a great diplomat. I know on the air he seems very pointed and specific—like a laser beam—when he's addressing topics. But there's more. Behind the scenes he has an amazing way of coming at things from various points of view and with a lot of nuance. He's not just superfast on his feet intellectually, he's also wise. That's a powerful combination.

Working with Greg is like being on a rollercoaster that never stops. The guy is a nonstop comedy machine who's not afraid to take risks and push the envelope. But don't let all the laughs fool you—Greg is also a sharp political commentator who knows his stuff. He's not afraid to take on tough issues and he always has a unique perspective that keeps the conversation fresh and interesting.

The best thing about working with Greg, though, is that he's not afraid to be himself. He's authentic, and that's something you don't always see in this business. He's not trying to be anyone else; he's just Greg. That's why I respect him, and that's why people love him.

I've already mentioned Dana but there's no way I'm not talking about her more. From the day I arrived, she has extended the hand of friendship and mentorship. Although I don't fit under any wing imaginable that she could have, she's taken me under her wing, and it has served me well. First of all, it's *Doctor* Dana, because I was given the honor of doing the story of her receiving her doctorate on *The Five*. I thought, *What an amazing cap to what has already been an amazing career.* She's a role model for anybody aspiring to be their best selves. Every time I'm on *America's Newsroom* or *The Five* and have the chance to sit next to her, I'm learning something.

Dana served as the White House Press Secretary under President George W. Bush, which is no small feat. That kind of high-pressure job requires a level of skill and poise that most people can only dream of. And she's brought that same level of expertise to her work as a news commentator. But it's not just her experience that makes her a pro. Dana has a way of breaking down complex issues in ways that make them easy to understand. She's got a way with words that's both intelligent and accessible—a rare talent in the world of news commentary. Plus, she's not afraid to ask the tough questions and challenge conventional wisdom. That's what makes her a standout in her field.

Another thing that sets her apart is her personality. Dana is just plain likable. She's got a sense of humor that's infectious, and she's always quick with a smile or a laugh. That kind of warmth and approachability goes a long way in building a connection with the audience and everyone she interacts with.

And her work ethic... Dana is a true professional who takes her job seriously. She's always well-prepared and well-informed. She never phones it in. Whether she's on camera or off, she's always giving 110 percent.

Let's talk about style. Dana has a way of presenting herself that's both professional and approachable. She's always impeccably dressed but never comes off as stuffy or aloof. That kind of balance is hard to achieve, but she makes it look easy.

Dana Perino is the real deal. She's a pro's pro, and one of the best in the business. Whether she's breaking down complex issues, cracking a joke, or just being herself, she's always on top of her game. When she speaks her mind you never get the sense that she's attacking anyone. She's fair-minded like that. If she disagrees with what you're doing, she gives you different sides and perspectives, in addition to her own opinion, so that you have a complete view of what's going on and where she's coming from. There's just something about her—you have to listen to what she's saying. There's a reason she's looked at as a leader at the network. And for someone of her stature, she's incredibly open and available. She's always there when you need here. She's probably my ultimate role model these days. You just want to carry yourself in the way that she carries herself.

Adding to the list of accomplished, intelligent, and powerful women at Fox News, I totally enjoy working with Judge Jeanine Pirro. She's another person, like Dana, who has extended her wing over me to help me adapt and grow.

First of all, let's talk about her legal background. Judge Jeanine is a former prosecutor and judge, so she knows the law inside and out. That kind of expertise is invaluable when it comes to analyzing legal issues and breaking down complex cases for the audience. Plus, she's not afraid to call out the BS when she sees it, and that's a rare quality in the world of legal commentary.

But it's not just her legal background that makes her a pro. Judge Jeanine has a presence on camera that's undeniable. She's got that no-nonsense attitude that comes from years of experience in the courtroom, paired with a quick wit and sense of humor that keeps things interesting. When she's on the air, you can't help but pay attention.

Another thing that sets her apart is her fearlessness. She's not afraid to take on controversial topics and speak her mind, regardless of what anyone else thinks. She's a strong, confident woman who knows her worth, and that kind of attitude is infectious. And let's not forget about her passion. Judge Jeanine cares deeply about the issues she discusses on her show, and that passion comes through in every segment. Whether she's talking about politics, law, or current events, you can tell she truly cares about getting to the heart of the matter and making a difference in the world.

Judge Jeanine has a presence on camera that's hard to describe. She's got an energy and a charisma that draws you in and keeps you hooked. And her delivery is always on point. She knows how to convey information in a way that's easy to understand, without ever dumbing it down. That's a rare talent, and it's what makes her stand out from the pack. Even when you don't want to hear it, she'll tell you what you need to know. I've learned so much about fighting for truth and what you believe in by getting to know her. I often imagine what it was like when she was a prosecutor in New York. I would never want to be on the wrong side of that cross-examination. I would be all, "Just give me a blank piece of paper and I'll sign on the bottom and put in whatever you want in. Just let me go. I'll do my time but I do not want to be cross-examined by her." I know some people think that the judge can sometimes come off as aggressive, but *so what*? That just means she's not afraid to tell it like it is. She may go hard sometimes but she also has the ability to demonstrate softness and compassion and give you the advice that you need to be a better person. She's always up-front. If I ask her a question and she doesn't have time to deal with it that day, she will tell me, "I don't have time today. I've got a million things going on. But I will look at it next week." And I know that when she does finally look at it, she's going to give me a complete and informed take. She tutors me sometimes, and I love that. Like a great coach, she gives you the tools you need to succeed.

Harris Faulkner? Pure journalistic integrity. She's amazing. She just has a way of telling the story. What a career, too. Started as a reporter and anchor for various local news stations, including WNCT-TV in Greenville, North Carolina, and WDAF-TV in Kansas City, Missouri, and later worked for the CBS News and ABC News networks before joining Fox News in 2005. She's won six Emmy Awards. She's also the author of several books.

I remember doing a show with her one time and we had a long break. We're supposed to come back and talk about reparations, but Kevin McCarthy came on unexpectedly to talk about the debt ceiling. That conversation went nine minutes and ran over my segment. I was expecting to get the boot, but she said to her producer, "No, I'm keeping Tyrus here for the next segment." I know the producer was saying, "Well, what's Tyrus going to say?" And she said, "You don't have to worry about him. He can say anything."

Look, I get that not everybody's a fan, but Harris let that producer know she had faith in me staying in that seat for an extended time. That meant a lot to me. Next, they flew in a story about the USS *Intrepid*, but the visual was wrong. They had the USS *Wasp* up there on the monitor. With only a small portion of the ship visible on the screen, she could tell it was wrong. She said, "You need to change that. That's not the *Intrepid*, that's the USS *Wasp*." She could barely see any of the ship on the screen and she knew that. She could see just three bolts on the side of a ship and know the name of it? Phenomenal, those little things that you see behind the scenes. She's one of several truly amazing news people at the network.

Take Bret Baier. When my first book came out and he wanted to have me on his show to talk about it, I couldn't believe it. Bret Baier? He talks to presidents. He's brilliant. He's insightful. What does he want with me? He has this move. After he reads something and he takes his glasses off, you know something big is about to go down. When the glasses come off, that's the gloves coming off. He's going to hit you with something serious.

So, he read a portion of my book out loud—an emotional part where I address my parents. When he finished reading, the glasses came off. I didn't know what was coming next, but he hit me with unexpected praise, saying that what I'd written was "powerful stuff, and deep stuff." Then it hit me. I was being addressed as an author. He was taking me seriously. That was the moment, the first time it really hit me: I was now an author. Automatically, this became one of the highlights of my life. I was just pinching myself. I'm sitting on set with one of the last great news men in the business. And he certainly is. You don't know what his personal opinions are when it comes to politics, because that's not what he does. He gives you the news and is just an amazing guy.

I also have to mention Charles Payne. He's best known for his work as a host and commentator on Fox Business, where he hosts the daily program *Making Money with Charles Payne*. He is also a contributor to Fox News, where he appears on various programs to discuss business and economic issues. He began his career on Wall Street as an analyst and worked for several investment firms before founding his own firm, Wall Street Strategies. In addition to his work on television, he's also the author of several books.

But, for me, when it comes to Charles, it's all about the clothes. His suit game is so strong I can't even think about ever wearing a suit. You never want to go up against him. His watch game isn't far behind. On top of all that, he's brilliant. He breaks down financial matters so that you understand things no matter what your experience level may be as a viewer. If you've never even heard of Wall Street, he will make sure you understand what's going on. But he can also sit with the greatest financial minds in the world and go toe to toe. Charles Payne is the kind of guy you want your kids to be like—always positive and always helpful. I just can't get enough of this guy.

You want to surround yourself with people who make you want to step up, never step down. Charles is that person. Bret is that person. Harris is that person.

And, oh yeah, Harold Ford Jr. He has a long legacy in politics. Former member of the United States House of Representatives from Tennessee, the son of former Congressman Harold Ford Sr., and the nephew of former Tennessee Senator John Ford. A member of the Democratic Party, he served in the House of Representatives from 1997 to 2007, representing Tennessee's 9th congressional district. After leaving politics, Ford Jr. worked as a commentator for

MSNBC and as a managing director at Morgan Stanley. Then we got him.

A class individual, and so profound, every time he speaks everybody stops to listen. I don't care how conservative you may be, he's always making sense. He's such a great debater, but never divisive. He's all about, "How do we stitch together our points of view into something productive?" Harold, if you're reading this right now, I wish you would go back in office. Not that I want to get rid of you at Fox—we just need you right now. Somebody with your intelligence and fair-mindedness is so necessary when it comes to making sense of what's happening in the world today. If you ever go that route, I will support you 100 percent.

I cannot *not* talk about Johnny Joey Jones. Some background: He joined the United States Marine Corps in 2005 and served for eight years, including three tours of Iraq and Afghanistan. During his service, he was deployed as an Explosive Ordnance Disposal (EOD) technician and was severely injured in 2010 while clearing IEDs in Afghanistan, resulting in the loss of both of his legs above the knee and severe damage to his right forearm and both hands.

After his retirement from the military, right around the time I joined, Jones became a political commentator and a frequent contributor to Fox News. He shares his insights on national security, veterans' issues, and other political topics. He is also a motivational speaker, sharing his inspiring story of resilience and perseverance in the face of adversity. Jones has been involved in various charitable organizations that support veterans and their families, including the Boot Campaign, the EOD Warrior Foundation, and the Gary Sinise Foundation. I *love* this guy. Not only is Johnny a true American hero who served our country with honor and distinction, but he's also an inspiration to everyone around him. Despite the injuries he sustained while serving in the military, Johnny never feels sorry for himself. He has a positive attitude that's infectious, and it's impossible not to feel inspired when you're around him.

Johnny and I bonded right out of the gate. I believe it was the first time he was on *Gutfeld!*, and he made a joke about losing his legs. I thought it was funny, but the crowd didn't know how to respond. It was awkward. I get that. It's not a normal thing to joke about, but there he was. He didn't care. And if he didn't care, why should anybody else care? I looked out at the crowd and said, "If he's making fun of it, if he has enough courage to actually make light of what he's been through, then you all better have the damn decency to laugh." And they did. From that point on, anytime he came on the show, he and I would go back and forth.

Me: *You don't have a leg to stand on.*
Him: *No, but I can fold mine up.*

That became part of our chemistry. This dude made such an impression on me. I've learned so many lessons from his behavior. He's a fighter, and he never gives up. He's faced some of the toughest challenges imaginable, but he's never let that stop him from achieving his goals and helping others along the way. It's a pleasure to work with Johnny. He's a true professional who always brings his A-game.

But what I really admire about Johnny is his positive attitude. He's always looking for the silver lining, and he never lets his injuries define who he is. Instead, he uses his experiences to inspire others and make a positive impact in the world. Johnny Joey Jones is an inspiration to everyone around him and a pleasure to work with. I have so much respect for this guy, and I'm honored to call him my friend. Despite the challenges he has faced, Johnny Joey Jones is known for his positive attitude, unwavering determination, and commitment to helping others. He's a beloved and respected figure in the military and political communities.

I also need to take a moment to talk about my good buddy Brian Kilmeade, the hardest working man in the business. He's always up at the crack of dawn and the last to leave on Fridays. He's a true news man, with lots of street credibility. I've enjoyed reading his books, especially the one about Frederick Douglass and Abraham Lincoln. He's got a soft humor about him that really shines through. Plus he's a great interviewer. He and Greg have a fun kind of on-air competition between them, which is always entertaining because both guys are so damn smart.

But what I really appreciate about Brian is his straight-up level of truth. He wants everyone to do well, and he's not afraid to support young guys coming up. He's confident in his own abilities, and he wants the next generation to do well. When I first started out, Brian made me feel so damn comfortable. He would ask great questions and just made me feel at home.

And the thing about Brian is, he can play every position in the news business. He's like a utility player, always ready to step in and get the job done. He can do anything! He's got his own show, he's filling in for others, he's all over the place. The guy can do it all. He's a top-notch interviewer with great insights into politics and current events—not to mention a natural charisma that draws people in. He's up early, he's on top of things, and he's always ready to jump in and get the job done. He's like the Swiss Army knife of news commentators. He's got all the tools, and he knows how to use them.

As much as I learn from the hosts that I work with, sometimes, it's about the guests and regulars we have on that also help me see the world differently. One of those people who has had a deep influence on me is the great author, Walter Kirn. This guy is the kind of writer who makes you sit up and take notice. He's got a way with words that is off the charts. On top of that, he's got a perspective on the world that is both unique and deeply insightful.

I first met Walter when he was a guest on our show, and let me tell you, I was blown away. We hit it off immediately, and it was clear to me that this was a guy who had a lot to say and knew how to say it.

I first read Walter's novel *Up in the Air* when it came out, and I loved it. The way he captured the essence of corporate culture, the way he depicted the loneliness and isolation of a life on the road...it was something special. Then I read *Thumbsucker*, and I was hooked. The way he captured the angst and confusion of adolescence...it was like he was speaking directly to me, you know? But it was *Blood Will Out* that really got to me. It's a memoir that tells the story of Walter's friendship with a man named Clark Rockefeller, who turned out to be a con artist and a murderer. The book chronicles Walter's gradual realization that the man he thought was his friend was actually a pathological liar who had assumed multiple identities over the years.

But here's the thing. It's not just his writing that makes him a fascinating and inspiring personality. It's the way Walter approaches the world. He's got this deep, abiding curiosity about everything around him. He's always asking questions, always pushing the boundaries of what he knows and what he thinks he knows. That's something that's deeply influenced me over the years.

I'm a guy who's always been interested in the world around me. I've always been curious, hungry to learn more. Meeting Walter, reading his books, and getting to know him as a friend, has only deepened that hunger.

So yeah, you could say that my friendship with Walter means a lot to me. And you could say that our occasional appearances together are something I truly cherish. But more than that, you could say that Walter Kirn has impacted the way I see the world, and for that, I will always be grateful. Dude even came to my house outside of New Orleans once and we had an amazing visit. He's always welcome.

Then there's Jesse Watters. Now, I know I like to joke around and say I want to punch him in the face, but that's just a term of endearment, you know? It's like brothers busting each other's chops.

Jesse is one of the hardest working guys I know. He started out as Bill O'Reilly's man in the street, and he's gone on to become a real backbone of Fox News. He has a dry sense of humor that I really appreciate, and he's not afraid to make fun of himself. At the same time, when he's making a point, he's not messing around.

Now, I know Jesse's got this Eddie Haskell smirk about him that makes you just want to knock his teeth out. But again, that's just a term of endearment, you know? There's something about that smirk that I can't help but love.

What I really appreciate about Jesse, though, is his integrity. This is a guy who's not afraid to speak his mind, and he's always willing to stand up for what he believes in. That's really important in this day and age.

So, yeah, Jesse Watters is my boy. We may joke around and rib each other a little bit, but at the end of the day, we're all on the same team, fighting for what we believe in. I wouldn't have it any other way.

Now, let me tell you about my co-pilot on the crazy train that is the Greg Gutfeld show—Kat Timpf. Working with Kat has been an absolute pleasure, and I don't say that lightly. She's a hard-working, intelligent, and hilarious individual who I have the utmost respect for. Kat works her ass off. She's always prepared and ready to go, whether it's for a segment on the show or a chapter in her book. And speaking of books, can we talk about how we both ended up on the *New York Times* bestseller list? I mean, who would have thought that two supposed "sidekicks" like us would end up there? But we did, and for her part, it's all thanks to Kat's tireless work ethic and dedication to her craft.

I also have to give it up for Kat's sense of humor. She's got this dry wit that just kills me every time. We've had some pretty hilarious moments on the show together, and I think a lot of that has to do with her ability to bring the funny in a way that's dry, understated and biting. But it's not just her humor that I appreciate—it's her intelligence, and her willingness to speak her mind. You see, Kat may just be the last living breathing legitimate libertarian on the planet. I mean, this girl is all about personal freedom and individual liberty, and she's not afraid to speak out on issues that matter to her. And let me tell you, it's not easy being a libertarian in today's political climate. But Kat stands firm in her beliefs, and I have total respect for her because of it.

I don't want to get too sappy here, but I have to say that I truly admire Kat. She's worked hard to get where she is, and she's done it all with a smile on her face. I think that's why we've grown so well together on the show. We both know what it's like to work hard and fight for what we believe in. And let's be real—we both bring our own unique brand of crazy to the show. I throw the blows and she drops the jokes. It just works. I think we both bring out the best in each other, and it's been amazing to watch our friendship grow alongside the show.

As I'm sitting here finishing this book, there's a lot going on with Fox News—like changes in terms of personnel. Some nights it feels like every other network is doing stories about what's happening at our place. Look, change happens all the time, whether it's entertainment, news, or sports. Your favorite quarterback gets traded, retires, or gets cut. The character you love on a show gets killed off or departs to do something else. Whatever the situation is, change happens and we all just have to roll with it. That's how it works.

Some of us retire and ride off into the sunset. (More often than not, it's a forced retirement.) Some of us wind up getting fired. That's the thing about being on television. It all goes by in a flash. Change is relentless, and there's not much you can do about it. I know viewers want their favorite person back on the air, and I understand that. It's just the nature of the beast. I'm the same way. When an actor I like leaves one of my favorite shows, I'm ready to write the network and beg them to bring that person back. Or it crushes me when one of my favorite sports heroes retires. But change happens and I'm a firm believer in focusing on what you can do yourself to get by. That's all it's about. Getting by. And in this business, you can't get too comfortable, especially if you can't connect with your audience. I've learned how important that is. There's no tenure in any of this. You're only as good as your last show. You're only as good as your last joke. Also, you can't believe in your own hype. You can never believe you're bigger than a network, either.

I appreciate this opportunity to work at Fox News. It's been one hell of a ride and I hope it lasts a long time. When I first started at Fox, I had no experience in the news industry. I was just a big dude with a big mouth and a lot of opinions. But the people at Fox saw something in me and gave me a chance. That chance has meant everything to me. Working at Fox has been one of the greatest experiences of my life. I've had the opportunity to work with some of the smartest, funniest, and hardest-working people in the industry. And, I have to say, I appreciate them all more than they know.

Now, I know that Fox News isn't everyone's cup of tea. We've got our fair share of critics, and I'm not going to pretend that we're perfect. But what I will say is that the people at Fox are some of the most fair and balanced people you'll ever meet. We're not here to push an agenda or spout propaganda—we're here to give you the news, and to give you our opinions on that news. And we do it all with honesty and integrity.

When I started at Fox, I was a bit of a wild card. I had a reputation for being a bit...unpredictable. I credit Suzanne Scott for seeing something I didn't yet know was in me. Suzanne is the CEO of Fox News, a position she's held since May 2018. However, her career at Fox News began more than two decades ago, when she joined the network as a programming assistant in 1996.

Over the years, she worked her way up through the ranks, holding various positions at the network, including Senior Vice President of Programming and Development, Executive Vice President of Programming, and President of Programming. During this time, she played a key role in the development and success of some of Fox News's most popular shows, including *The O'Reilly Factor, Hannity & Colmes,* and *Fox & Friends.* Now, she is responsible for overseeing all aspects of Fox News and Fox Business Network, including programming, editorial content, and business operations. Under her leadership, the network has continued to be the most-watched cable news network in the United States.

Suzanne Scott is a true leader who knows how to get things done. She's has a sharp mind and a no-nonsense attitude that keeps everyone focused on the task at hand. When she sets her sights on a goal, she doesn't stop until it's achieved. And let me tell ya, that kind of drive and determination is infectious. It makes you want to work harder and be better.

But what really sets Suzanne apart is her commitment to the people who work for her. She's always looking out for us and making sure we have everything we need to succeed. Whether it's providing us with the resources we need to do our jobs or just being there to offer support and guidance, Suzanne is always there.

After just about three or four appearances on *Gutfeld!,* Suzanne sat me down for a meeting and said lots of positive things, including, "I think you have at least three books in you and a hit show." Well, let's just say I never thought I would be hearing that, especially from somebody as talented and accomplished as Suzanne. She is always giving me the opportunity and inspiration to be myself. "Just be Tyrus. Let's find out who Tyrus is." She sees plenty of things in me—things that I would never see myself. It's an incredible feeling to know that she doesn't just see your potential, but also encourages it and expects it.

Working at Fox has given me a platform to speak my mind, to share my opinions, and to make people laugh. I don't take that platform for granted. I know there are a lot of people out there who would kill for the opportunity to do what I do, and I'm grateful that I get to do it every day. But here's the thing: I wouldn't be where I am today without the people around me. I've been fortunate enough to work with some of the most talented and dedicated people in the industry, and they've all played a crucial role in my success. They've welcomed me with open arms, and have given me chances that nobody else would think of giving me. They've believed in me when nobody else did, and for that, I'm forever grateful.

In closing, it's been a wild ride putting together my new book. I'm beyond grateful to all of you who've taken the time to read it. Whether you're a die-hard fan or a curious skeptic, your support means the world to me. Even if you don't agree with everything I say, I still appreciate the hell out of you for reading it. We live in a world where people are so quick to dismiss others who don't see things exactly the same way they do. But that's not what this book is about. It's about opening up a dialogue, getting people to think, and maybe even challenging some long-held beliefs.

I'm not saying I have all the answers. Hell, I don't even have all the questions. But what I do know is that we're all in this together, whether we like it or not. And if we're going to make any progress as a society, we need to be willing to have some uncomfortable conversations. My hope is that my book can be a starting point for some of those conversations.

So, thank you for being open-minded. Thank you for being willing to hear me out, and most of all, thank you for being a part of this ongoing conversation about the future of our country.

Until next time, keep on keeping on. And remember, it's okay to disagree. It's okay to have different opinions. But let's always strive to listen to each other, respect each other, and maybe even learn a thing or two from each other. That's not just what makes this country great...that's what makes us human.

Nuff said.

Afterword

Well, well, well, look who made it to the end of my book! You must be a glutton for punishment, or maybe you just appreciate a good story or two. Either way, I appreciate you taking the time to read all about my stories and my take on the world.

Let's face it, the world can be a crazy place. From politics to pop culture, there's always something happening that makes you scratch your head and say, "What the hell is going on?"

Now, some of you might not agree with everything I've had to say in these pages. And that's fine. In fact, I encourage it. We need more people who are willing to have honest, open discussions about the issues that affect us all. Too many folks these days are quick to take offense or shut down opposing viewpoints, but that's not how we make progress.

So, to all the readers out there who've stuck with me through thick and thin, I want to say thank you. Thank you for being open-minded enough to listen to what I have to say, even if you don't always agree with it. Thank you for being willing to engage in meaningful conversations about the issues that matter.

I've had the pleasure of meeting some truly amazing people in my life, and many of them have shaped my worldview in ways I never could have imagined. From coaches to broadcasters, friends and family, I've been lucky enough to learn from some of the best.

And of course, I wouldn't be where I am today without all of you. You are the reason I do what I do, and I'll never forget that. Whether you're tuning in to my shows, reading my books, or just following me on social media, I couldn't be more grateful.

So, as we bring this book to a close, I want to leave you with a few parting words. First and foremost, don't be afraid to speak your mind. We need more people who are willing to stand up for what they believe in, even if it's not the popular opinion. And secondly, always keep a sense of humor about you. Life's too short to take everything so seriously. Sometimes, the best thing you can do is laugh.

With that said, I'll wrap things up by saying once again, thank you. Thank you for your support, your feedback, and your willingness to engage in honest, open discussions about the issues that matter. And who knows, maybe we'll cross paths again someday. Until then, keep fighting the good fight.

Nuff said.

Acknowledgments

In my first book, I acknowledged many people that had a major influence in my life given the scope of the story. For this title, I'm keeping it simple.

I'd like to thank Dana Perino and Billy Corgan for contributing their forewords. I am humbled by your words and thank you both for your professionalism and friendship.

I'd like to thank Anthony Ziccardi and Jacob Hoye from Post Hill Press for taking a chance on me, not just once, but twice. Both of our deals have been old school—a hand shake. These are two men of their words, a rarity to say the least, and I hope they are as proud of this book as they were of the first one.

And to my writing coach and consigliere Chris Epting, aka "Alfred," thank you for yet another awesome journey. *Just Tyrus* and *Nuff Said*... What's next ????

About the Author

A 6'8", 350-pound behemoth, Tyrus is an affable, hard-working entertainer with a sly sense of humor. Following his initial calling to football, he became a bouncer at numerous establishments in Los Angeles where he caught the attention of Snoop Dogg and became his bodyguard. That drew the attention of the WWE where he went on to enjoy success as "Brodus Clay," and later, "The Funkasaurus," which led to his starring in Mattel commercials and appearing in WWE videogames. Along with working as an actor in film and television, he recently captured the NWA Worlds Heavyweight Championship and is a co-host of American's number one late-night comedy, *Gutfeld!* He is the author of the *New York Times* bestseller, *Just Tyrus*.